Mr Berger
you have a
clever personality
but you, have a heart
Berger!
hope you enjoy reading
this

Best Wishes
[signature]

Born on the
Wrong Side

Born on the Wrong Side

by

CEC THOMPSON

The Pentland Press
Edinburgh – Cambridge – Durham – USA

First published in 1995 by
The Pentland Press Ltd
1 Hutton Close,
South Church
Bishop Auckland
Durham

All photographs in this book
come from the author's private collection

ISBN 1-85821-339-8

Typeset by Carnegie Publishing, 18 Maynard St, Preston
Printed and bound by Bookcraft, Bath

Contents

Acknowledgements

There are so many people I need to thank for their help with this book. First, I shall be eternally grateful to Richard Burns, novelist of promise and potential and a former colleague of mine at Chesterfield Grammar School, who died tragically young. His inspiration got me started and he was always there in my mind's eye as the book took shape.

I must also thank Robert Gate, the Rugby League historian, whose fund of research material covering both codes of rugby has been enormously helpful to me; also Billy Burgess, Paul Charlton, Ellery Hanley, Andy Key, Ike Southward, Alan Tait and David Watkins, as well as my Australian friends and former colleagues, Bill McCall, Bev Wilson and the late Johnny Mudge, all former or current players. Their help has proved invaluable.

In the academic world, Professors Maurice Beresford, John Chartres and Roy Wilkinson and senior lecturers John Brothwell, George Rainee and Ken Woolmer have given me the benefit of their scholarly minds. Mrs Salisbury read the final manuscript and made useful contributions, corrections and suggestions. Harry Jepson, formerly a director, now a vice-president, of Leeds RLFC and a director of the Rugby Football League, with his encyclopaedic knowledge of the game, was also enthusiastically at my beck and call.

I must also thank David Howes, formerly the public relations executive of the Rugby Football League; Bev Risman, Andrew Cudbertson and Jack Abernethy of the Student Rugby League; Dick Viney; John Morgan of the *Yorkshire Evening Post* and John Walsh of the *Workington Times & Star*; Mike Green, an unfailing source of information about Hunslet RLFC; and my brother Bob for his store of memorabilia regarding our parents and siblings.

I am also most grateful to Tony Pocock, who has influenced the shape and content of the book from beginning to end and made me believe that my personal recollections would be of interest to the general reader; Lynne Cook and Ros Sanderson, each of whom has endlessly typed and retyped the manuscript; and above all my wife Anne and my son Mark, who have endured with exemplary patience the hours I have spent alone in my study writing and rewriting.

Cockermouth,   Cec Thompson
May 1995

Foreword

BY DAVID OXLEY OBE,

FORMERLY CHIEF EXECUTIVE,

THE RUGBY FOOTBALL LEAGUE

Theodore Cecil Thompson is one of the most remarkable men I have been privileged to meet. Born of a black father, who died before Cec was born, and a courageous, proud but reserved white mother, with whom he could never converse, he suffered a succession of orphanages and soul-destroying dead-end jobs before, by chance, he found the game of Rugby League football, at which he came to excel and which changed the whole course of his life.

In the late 1940s and throughout the 1950s, Cec played outstandingly well for Hunslet and Workington Town and was capped for Great Britain, against New Zealand, in 1951. I didn't know and never met Cec Thompson, the man, at that time. I knew him simply as an avid sports fan believes he knows the player on the park – and in Cec's case that meant pace, power and perpetual motion. He was one of the few great Rugby League forwards of yesteryear who could have translated to the modern game with no need radically to change his style of play. How we roared at our players to 'get a grip of Darkie', our entreaties not rooted in racism but indicative of the respect, admiration and, indeed, affection we all felt for the superbly lithe athlete who was dominating the match. How we wanted him in *our* pack!

Nevertheless, success on the field did little to assuage Cec's deep-rooted sense of inferiority, inadequacy and social unease, usually hidden behind brash behaviour and, at times, over-the-top ebullience. It did, however, awaken his belief, soon to become a burning conviction, that self-improvement was possible no matter how disadvantaged one's background and that a concentrated formal education, denied him in his early years, was the key to all self-advancement. The extraordinary strength, stamina and doggedness which characterised Cec's play were to become the decisive factors in his quest for education and the benefits his driven soul knew it would bring him.

Money he had earned from the game bought Cec a window-cleaning round. Hard work and hitherto unsuspected business acumen transformed the round into a profitable enterprise. Income from the business saw Cec through college, the slog of acquiring necessary 'O' and 'A' levels and, ultimately, the award of an honours degree in economics, followed by a diploma in education, at Leeds University.

His career at Leeds was 'the best of times and the worst of times'. His obsession with education meant that for eight critical years academic studies took strict precedence over all other activities, all relationships. Enthusiasm ('my greatest ally in life'), the encouragement of some good friends and, above all, the steadfast devotion of Anne, his wife, an unfailing support through all those years, carried him through.

It had been a tough and bloody road for him. Betrayed by a business partner, on the edge of mental breakdown more than once, coping with a divorce and remarriage, near penury, arraigned on a false charge of assaulting a pupil, Cec survived and prospered to achieve the self-advancement he craved and the self-fulfilment we all seek. He had discovered an innate talent for helping others towards self-improvement which made him a natural teacher, though a hard taskmaster who could never understand nor tolerate lack of personal ambition in his pupils.

Just as in Rugby League, the complete newcomer, press-ganged into making up the numbers in a works tournament, blossomed into a full Great Britain international, so the stumbling, self-conscious youth, who had to print his name when Rugby League fans asked for his autograph, transformed himself into the highly regarded, outstandingly successful head of economics at Chesterfield Grammar School. And then, in 1994, he was the recipient of an honorary master's degree from his old university for his services to the community.

This is the moving, thought-provoking, inspirational story of one

man's successful battle to find his true self, a man in whom there is
no hate, no aggression, only dignity and self-respect. Though residual
feelings of unease and inadequacy still occasionally arise, there is no
doubt that Theodore Cecil Thompson can now more than hold his
own at any level of society. Those of us who are fortunate enough to
enjoy his friendship are invariably warmed and enlightened by the
experience – just as readers of this fascinating book will be too.

Harrogate,   David Oxley
May 1995

PART I

WALKING

Chapter 1

I didn't know I was a 'nigger' until I was twelve. Since my father, William Alfred Thompson, was a full-blooded black from Port of Spain, Trinidad that may be a bit surprising. He was born in 1887 only a few yards from the Red House, the parliament building of Trinidad and Tobago. Aged only thirty-nine, he died in Leeds a few months before I was born, in 1926, in County Durham. So I never saw my father and though I suppose I realised, as I grew up, that the colour of my skin was not the same as that of other children, I was well into my boyhood before I realised that in others' eyes I was 'different'.

The year I was born my eldest brother, Robert, was seven. He remembers our father as a tall handsome man who attracted people's attention the moment he walked into a room. The few photographs I have seen of him show an impeccably groomed black Edwardian in a wing collar, with a gold watch and chain adorning his waistcoat and a handkerchief in his top pocket. I suppose his surname must have been that of some British plantation owner who had imposed his patronym on the slaves in his possession, but my father was a proud free man.

He was a master painter-decorator by trade, and he came to England, as a corporal in the British West Indies Regiment, during the First World War. His battalion, the 5th Reserve, had been in Egypt, but he was later posted to County Durham. After the war, rather than returning to Trinidad – where his sister was a teacher and his brother a qualified lawyer – he remained in England, in Birtley, because he had fallen in love.

The woman he loved, the woman who was to become my mother, was Florence Greenwell. She was a miner's daughter: perhaps she was used to men with black faces. It certainly was an unusual alliance for

3

that time but there is no doubt that she was devoted to my father, and soon they had a thriving family. Apart from my brother Bob, there was our sister Linda, and another brother, Aubrey. My father had won a contract to put gold leaf on the walls of the Leeds Town Hall, and it was in Leeds that I was conceived. With the job came a house, and comparative prosperity. But sand had got into my father's spleen during his time in Egypt and he died and was buried in Armley, a suburb of Leeds, before I was born.

I think my mother was about twenty-six when my father died. Not only had her father been a miner but no less than six of her brothers (there were ten children altogether) had become miners on leaving school. Now she was left destitute with four young children all under the age of seven. Just after my father was buried the bailiff came round because Linda's pram had been bought on credit and now there was no more money coming in to pay off the instalments. More important, the house was forfeit, being ours only because of my father's job.

My poor mother: she lost her husband, she lost her house, and she got me. She travelled up to Durham to be with her family for my birth, and then returned to Leeds, but she couldn't cope on her own with all of us. Indeed, her life was in tatters. What was to become of her children? Where could shelter be found? How could they be fed? Where could she go? It was then, as she tried to face up to this appalling dilemma, that the Waifs and Strays Society came to her rescue.

All my life, even when I had hardly a penny to my name, I have supported the Waifs and Strays. I shall never forget how they helped my mother and all the benefits I received from my fostering and orphanage upbringing. All four of my mother's children were sent to various orphanages around the country. Bob went to Merseyside, Aubrey to Kent and I, a tiny baby only a few months old, was fostered in Warminster in Wiltshire. Because we were scattered like that my mother could not afford to visit us too often. When she did come to see me I had no real idea who she was, this tall, dark, handsome lady with her proud bearing and kind, intelligent face. My sister Linda was the most fortunate since my mother eventually took a position as housekeeper to a Mr Bonner, a property dealer, at his bungalow in Stanningley, a suburb of Leeds, and Linda was sent to St Chad's orphanage in Headingley.

Warminster furnishes me with my earliest memories. My foster mother was a Mrs Taylor and she had a terraced house on the common. She was, presumably, a widow, possibly in her mid-forties, with a grown-up daughter in her late teens or early twenties. Each morning my surrogate mother went through a ritual of persistent struggle to get her daughter out of bed to go to work. Mrs Taylor was clean, tidy and caring, but as a substitute mother, the relationship quite under-standably stopped short of loving. I was never kissed nor lovingly caressed. At Warminster I learned to spell 'put' on my first day at school, I remember, and I was frightened of the gypsies who came round selling pegs.

This clinically clean home possessed nothing of any cultural interest, no books or pictures, no newspapers or radio which might connect the household to the world at large, though Mrs Taylor did tell me ghost stories during winter nights, sitting before a coal fire, and those I loved. In her closeted world she seemed content to let the universe pass her by, and with her I was happy, warm and well-fed, and came to no harm. Like the mining community into which I had been born, she had real pride in cleanliness though Warminster was a blissful, rustic environment in total contrast to the stern community of the colliers. Those were my smiling pumpkin days.

However, though well-fed and cared for, I received no preparation for school from Mrs Taylor nor did I learn to mix with other people since I don't remember visitors ever coming to the house. So I was well on the way to becoming the ponderous, slow-thinking, pretty hopeless good-for-nothing which characterised the first twenty years of my life. When presented with any sort of problem, I seemed always to be at a disadvantage. My mind simply would not function. I had no fixed habits to go by, nothing to get hold of, nowhere to start from. I was helpless throughout my teenage years when it came to understanding or learning and was totally lacking in confidence.

It seems odd but I do not recall actually leaving Warminster for my first orphanage in Weston-super-Mare in Somerset at the age of five, and have preserved only one memory from that time. Some sports event or other had taken place and the youngsters from the orphanage were put in line, and like a sad, advancing army moved across the field to collect the litter which had been carelessly discarded by the crowd.

My next orphanage at Tattenhall, in Cheshire, revealed the first signs of puberty; I fell in love. Her name was Helen and she had a wonderful smile. She lived close to the orphanage and went to the same school as me. She had abundant charm and was good looking with long flowing black hair, lustrous when the sun shone upon it, and had exquisite eyes. She was the first to arouse my sexual impulses and, since I never mixed socially, I remained true to her throughout my teenage years! I rarely spoke to her and took only sidelong looks at her beauty, terrified that she might object to my stolen glances and to my finding her so breathtakingly lovely. Perhaps my proudest moment in those years at Tattenhall arrived during a village carnival. The orphanage entered a float and I took the part of an Indian prince. In that guise perhaps I would be able to win Helen's love, I thought.

The orphanages at Weston and Tattenhall were secure places. The food was plain but wholesome and I was kept clean and cheerful. Porridge made with water and sprinkled with salt provides a sound breakfast. I remember also boiled fish and potatoes, rice pudding, and bread with jam or dripping. We grew vegetables, mended our own clothes and helped to keep the place clean. I learned to darn socks, and generally to take care of my things. Life was plain but good, and though we may not have received the love and affection a child brought up in a family might expect, we never missed what we had never known.

It was in 1937 that I moved to my last orphanage, in Tynemouth, where my life's troubles began. Grey shorts, stockings and shirts, and grey sweaters in winter, made it pretty obvious who were the boys from the orphanage in the school we attended. My brown skin made me even more conspicuous until I felt I was shining like a Belisha Beacon. My timid nature encouraged the other boys to make me a target for their bullying. They used to form a circle round me and then push me round and round, making me ricochet faster and faster until I was hurtling round the encircling bodies. My shirt would always get torn as I was grabbed and then hurled away, the gang hilarious from seeing this wretched coon becoming increasingly dizzy and woe-begone.

At the orphanage, any boy with a torn garment was caned. A ritual took place in which I bent over a chair while the boys sat round the perimeter of the main hall to witness the caning. I was too shy and too terrified to try to explain my innocence. I became more and more introverted as the regular canings continued, and as my rage at the unfairness of the punishment was bottled tight inside me. I was inexpressibly miserable and longed for my time at orphanage and school to end. Those dreadful years at Tynemouth created in me a pattern of behaviour which lasted throughout my teens and had a permanent effect on my life.

A few disconnected meaningless images remain from that monotonous time. For some reason I have a vivid memory of a public house sign – the Dolphin – set at a T-junction on Linskill Road, diagonally opposite my dormitory, in a world still largely beyond my comprehension. During the days before Christmas we would sing carols outside the big posh houses, collecting money to buy presents for each other. We attended church each Sunday, a dull service which meant nothing to any of us. In the afternoon, we enjoyed the luxury of three caramels each. Another treasured memory was being able to swim for the first time in the open-air swimming pool on Tynemouth shore.

In later life I realised that the Tynemouth orphanage was close to where I was born and where my maternal grandparents and many other relations lived. It seems strange that we should never have met or tried to meet, just as I often used to wonder why my mother or even her parents could not have taken care of me as a baby. I know that my mother was neither incompetent nor inadequate: it was simply grinding poverty that made it impossible for her to keep me at home even if Mr Bonner had allowed it. My grandparents, too, had no less than ten children, six brothers and four sisters. Shift work was vital for them; and with only three bedrooms to the house, all the beds were always occupied. This hand-to-mouth existence would have left no room to house my mother and her family of four. Moreover, my grandparents were constantly exhausted with never-ending domestic routines. A coal fire had always to be kept alight for it was essential for daily cooking and heating and for the bath water for washing. On top of this were regular never-ending pregnancies. There was simply no time and no money for any form of leisure. And you worked when you were ill to avoid bringing home reduced wages, a constant fear when living on the breadline.

Nonetheless, I did meet my grandparents for the first and only time in 1938, when I was twelve, the year I moved from Tynemouth back to Leeds when my mother remarried. How well I remember travelling from Leeds to Chester-le-Street on my own to meet them. My grandmother was still beautiful, though she had borne twelve children, and it was bliss when she crushed me to her chest. It was the most emotional moment of my young life, to be hugged and smothered with kisses for the first time. I could scarcely breathe but I was willing to die for her embraces. Now I recall the warmth of the love she showered on me then whenever I see parents hugging and kissing their children; and it is then that I understand fully what it means to be deprived of love. My grandmother burst out with the words, 'My son, my son, how much I love you.'

My grandfather, Matt Greenwell, a tall, erect, proud man, impeccably groomed in his immaculate single-breasted suit, a silver watch chain across his waistcoat, looked a grand figure. The bristles of his moustache scratched my skin as he kissed me, his strong arms almost engulfing me. The prickling discomfort was a joy, my first kiss ever from a man, and brought tears once again streaming down my face. I was getting my first taste of family life. Unashamedly, we gave vent to our emotions. But this was a mere morsel of the feast of emotion that was to come from numerous uncles and aunts when I reached the small mining village of Ouston, near Birtley, Chester-le-Street, in County Durham, where they lived.

Once everyone had settled back to their everyday routine, my grandfather asked, 'Well, Cecil, tell me about yourself, your journey, and about your life.' Though usually a person of few words, he was soon telling me about himself. My grandfather was a strong and dedicated family man. He was highly respected in the community and people came to him for advice. When he was formally dressed, he looked to me like a Victorian prince, a sensible, quiet-spoken man, honest and principled. Those few days of love, care and affection were among the most cherished moments of my early life. They made me realise how vitally important it is for children to be given a loving environment. To my great sadness, after this visit I never saw my grandfather again and when I heard in 1942 that he had died at the age of sixty-five, in the year of his retirement, after a lifetime in the local pit, and my grandmother a year or two later, I was devastated.

Ouston village consisted simply of lines of terraced houses with outside toilets down the middle of a dirt path between the rows. Squares of neatly cut newspaper hung on a nail for toilet paper and zinc baths were placed against the walls. In the kitchen, there was a brick construction for boiling water from a coal fire. This provided my grandfather with a hot bath six days a week after work to wash from his body the filth from toiling down below at the coal face. After fifty-one years of this unremitting routine, his health had taken a pounding. Stumbling through the morning mists to work miles underground, in conditions where movement was cramped by narrow tunnels, he would sweat at the coal face, frequently for ten hours at a stretch, in semi-darkness, and often in constant pain. Once he said to me, in the precious short time I was with him, 'Son, don't ever go down the mines.' He worked always saturated with sweat, with coal dust sticking to his body. In those dreadful conditions, the men's bait, potted meat sandwiches with cold tea, would be consumed half crouching in crevices, mice scuttling around their legs. At the end of each shift, there came the agonizing backward march to the lift, bent double for miles. They were born to accept scarred backs, and were often crippled by injury. My grandfather died of silicosis and there was never a penny of compensation. The mine owner was the ultimate gaffer over life and death.

The year I met my grandparents, 1938, was the year my mother remarried in Leeds. Her new husband was a baker called Edwin Tipling, born and bred in Leeds, and gradually they began to bring her children home. Linda had never left Leeds, so she was the first to rejoin them; I was the youngest, so I came next.

Mr Bonner lent my mother and Edwin enough money to open a bakery and confectionery shop in Meanwood, a pretty rough suburb of north-west Leeds. As in Birtley, there were long streets of back-to-back houses in those days, with outside toilets and not many dustbins. Edwin was a good man, a good baker and immensely hard working. Indeed, with Edwin's inspiration and my mother's administrative skills and parsimonious lifestyle, the bakery flourished.

I shall never forget 159 Meanwood Road, where we lived above the shop. The road carried a busy tramway from North Street, a commercial area in central Leeds, up to the terminus at the end of Meanwood Road. That was roughly a six-mile journey, and from 5.30 in the morning the trams would start to grind noisily past the house. No. 159 had four rooms, with an attic and a cellar which housed sacks of flour, jars of jam, bottles of fruit, boxes of currants and raisins, lard and so on. A section of the cellar contained coke for stoking the fire for baking the handmade confectionery.

There were two ground-floor rooms: the shop, which provided bread and confectionery for the concentration of back-to-back terrace houses in the immediate neighbourhood and sold cigarettes and sweets as well, and behind it the bakehouse, dominated by the ovens, each about three foot square, placed on top of a fireplace. From cellar floor to attic ceiling the heat from the ovens was sweltering. Moreover, every floorboard squeaked. So if I stayed out later than I should, there could be no clandestine sneaking in and up two flights of stairs. Above the shop was the lounge, used only at weekends or for visitors. But on the same floor as the lounge was my mother and stepfather's bedroom, which had been fitted with a bath, and occupants of the attic had to pass through it on the way to the spiral staircase to the top of the house. The attic was divided by a screen for privacy since each side could house a double-sized bed. Linda occupied one side and the other was mine. If I suddenly had to go to the toilet in the middle of the night, it meant a tricky passage down the spiral stairway, through my parents' bedroom, then down another flight of stairs to unlock the back door, and encounter whatever the elements offered – a raging gale, torrential rain or a freezing, icy path. Chamber pots were essential for a desperate pee in the night. There is talk of slopping out in prisons these days, but such was a daily ritual through the bakehouse. Health standards today would probably require the lowering of a bucket from the bedroom window. Life was certainly primitive and a terrifying change of culture from my protected orphanage environment. However, from time to time, as her children homed in on Leeds before going off to the war, my mother's determination to have all her four children under her roof if only for a day – though never, alas, together – was rewarded.

Bob came and went to Burma, sharing a bed with me on the way. Then Aubrey, in the RAF, and I shared that bed before I sailed away to Singapore in the Royal Navy. When I got home Bob had left to marry his first wife, Blanche, and Aubrey was pursuing his career as a singer. But my lasting memory of Meanwood Road is partly of the trams swaying past to release their occupants into the comparatively salubrious air of central Leeds and partly of my mother facing without flinching all that life could throw at her and winning through in the end.

Edwin had great integrity but no great intelligence and did little to guide me towards a worthwhile way of life. Out of the bakery he would enjoy two or three pints in the pub, lay a few bets, become absorbed briefly in the racing results, and enjoy the local gossip. My mother, too, who was a good deal more intelligent than Edwin, could do little to help me. She was too reserved and I was too stupid. We really had nothing whatever to say to each other. Though there was no lack of love, we could not communicate. Each Saturday evening she used to sit and almost complete the *Yorkshire Evening Post* crossword with the help of a dictionary for the more unusual words. But we rarely spoke.

The orphanages may have been simple and unsophisticated – so was I – but, except for my days at Tynemouth, they seemed like paradise compared with the new life I entered now. It was then that I found out that I was a 'nigger': 'Hi, nigger boy!' someone shouted at me, 'did you come out of your mother's arse?' Nor did it help that I was called Cecil: 'You a poofter then?' I felt like a budgerigar among sparrows.

In those days there were very few black people away from the seaports. Leeds is about as far from the sea as you can get, and I felt as if I had walked out of a freak show. I was an outcast, and I remember thinking back to the gypsies who had frightened me in Warminster. I had become a gypsy too, someone to frighten the children, to be pointed at, to be despised. For the first time in my life I started to wet the bed, which only increased my sense of inadequacy. Would I be persecuted for the rest of my life? Was there nowhere to hide? The only place in which I felt safe was the cinema – we were all the same colour in the dark. But the lights always came back on.

Nor was my pigmentation my only problem. I was a healthy child but there had never been any money in the orphanages for sports equipment, so what potential I had was undeveloped. And I had achieved nothing at school. 'Give me a child until he is seven and I will give you the man', goes the old saying. But I was allowed to drift. There were no speech-day prizes, no favourable reports for me. I never became a prefect or won anything on sports day. The only thing I had to be grateful for at that stage in my life was that I went to Blenheim School – though that was on Blackman Lane, a coincidence I could have done without – and not the closer but rougher Sheepscar School. My only ambition was to keep my head down to hide the colour of my skin; my only achievement was to learn how to fail. In short, I was simply passing from cradle to grave.

At the beginning of the war, because our school was commandeered for a barracks, I was evacuated to Sprotborough near Doncaster for a while. This gave me a short rustic holiday, but I was still wetting my bed and the people I was staying with couldn't cope, so I was soon back in Leeds. Worse, Blenheim School was still under military control, and I had no choice but to go to Sheepscar. Sheepscar School had an evil reputation, which it fully deserved. Future criminals did their training there, and the heroes were the gangleaders and pimps, characters out of *Brighton Rock*. I could so easily have drifted into the seedy style of life they aspired to, stealing, gambling, boozing, fast cars, fast chicks and the unsteady flit from pub to pub, prison to prison; perhaps the only thing that stopped me was that I was so shy.

I remember once travelling on a bus. Two teenage girls were sitting on the seat behind me. I happened to cough. 'Oo,' said one of the girls. 'They cough just like us, don't they?' Had I been articulate, had some trace of personality developed in me in those days, I might have thought of an answer.

With this sort of experience behind me it is hardly surprising that, by the time I left school at fourteen, I was utterly desensitised and virtually unemployable. For four more years, as the war raged, I blundered about from one blind-alley labouring job to another.

My first job after leaving school was as a moulderer's labourer, which consisted mainly of sieving sand with oil to be used for making moulds. Into these moulds molten metal was poured for the manufacture of all sorts of iron implements. I had a sit-up-and-beg bicycle and travelled from Meanwood Road over Leeds Bridge to my factory in Hunslet – a journey of some three miles. Many manual workers stay all their lives at their particular job, as a skilled moulderer, a furnaceman, a semi-skilled lorry driver, and so on. But I counted myself lucky to escape from that job, indeed from most of my jobs, though the departures were certainly not engineered. I was just drifting, bored stiff by each of them. Most of the work I did required absolutely no thought at all. My next job was 'running' in a textile mill, carrying lengths of cloth on my shoulder. I simply had to be pointed in a direction from A to B, and ran. I was just a beast of burden really, a clod hopper.

Another job consisted simply of moving suites of furniture around as skilled craftsmen worked on chairs and settees. I supplied them with their materials, took away finished products and stacked them into warehouses. Each evening vans had to be loaded for delivery to shops the next day. There were lots of such jobs available since most able-bodied men were in the forces. For a short while, too, I worked for Edwin, kneading dough, cleaning out bun-tins, icing cakes, putting cherries on macaroons, fuelling the ovens, delivering orders – a general dogsbody in other words. I hated it, being cooped up in one room all day. There weren't enough rooms in the house to live in without working in one of them.

So I took yet another job, this time at Kirkstall Forge on the outskirts of West Leeds, making rear axles for the lorries that would be needed on the battlefields of Europe. I was old enough to work on night shifts now and somehow this work sparked off explosive energy within me. Physical contact with the opposite sex had escaped me because I was, I suppose, alien. Admiring the girls in the local swimming-bath was the limit of my sexual experience. Now all my activity at Kirkstall Forge was like giving a can of spinach to Popeye. Strangely enough, I stopped having wet dreams; my energy was being daily absorbed.

I did this job for almost a year with a gang of eight men. It involved an eight-hour shift of continuous activity. One of us would feed a forged piece of metal into a furnace; it was then taken out at the other end of the furnace by another gang using a crane and put into a shaping machine. The heated metal would then be bored with a heavy rod and would become circular and elongated. This whole process would take some five minutes or so. The shaping machine would be opened up and I would grasp the end of the rod with rags in my hands and release it from the machine by striding backwards over a hard block of wood and taking one step to my left – a ballroom chassé. A guy with tongs would pull the reshaped metal out of the machine and it would slur over the block of wood and slide into a pit of water. Then I would chassé back in line with the machine, stride over the block and the whole process would be repeated.

Being on piece work, paid for the number of times we performed this operation, we became experts. It was the sort of job and the sort of life that had to be endured by millions of people on the factory floor, prisoners of monotony. But at least this ceaseless round of sweating toil made me fit and strong and loose-limbed, and I had discovered a new facet of myself – explosive energy. At the end of my shift I was too exhausted for any physical activity, sexual or otherwise. Sleep came to me the moment my head hit the pillow. Solid sleep of seven to nine hours built up reserves of energy which allowed another shift of furious activity the following day. At such times I became a kind of colossus. My body strength enabled me to perform spells of manual labour that were almost superhuman. I became a youth of truly enormous strength and power. Little did I realise that I was also being prepared for my rugby career in the years ahead.

Yet another job remains in my memory: on my first day in an engineering factory in Hunslet, during the lunch break, the roughnecks decided to taunt me. 'Cecil, is your prick black?' asked a particularly ugly youth. It seemed sensible to ignore this so I got on with eating my lunch. But this wasn't good enough. About five of them crowded round me and then suddenly jumped on me, ripping off my boiler suit, pulling down my trousers and underpants and pouring oil over my testicles. They were really enjoying themselves, laughing loudly in the process, but I didn't laugh. Maybe this was less racialism than irresponsible skylarking; nonetheless such wearisome behaviour at my expense was often the price of being black in a white society. I didn't have any more lunch that day: I spent the rest of the dinner-time in the toilet trying to clean myself, then left the job five hours after starting it. To be fair, this sort of thing didn't happen often, but even once is enough to leave scars. It was time to get away from Leeds. So

I took the only escape route, then available to a working-class lad, and volunteered for the Royal Navy. It was early in 1944.

The navy offered more than an escape. They would look after me, I thought, and after my orphanage years I dearly wanted that. And they would give me somewhere to dream. I had always been a dreamer. I imagined myself in naval uniform – so much more glamorous, I thought, than the army or RAF – and pictured myself seeing the world. But the world had to wait a while. The first place I saw was Portsmouth. Going to Portsmouth took me through London, a dangerous and sophisticated place. Walking between stations I was stopped by a charming man, well-groomed and well-spoken, who wondered if I wanted a drink. I was nice looking, if the photographs are to be believed, and I was naive. 'How delightful,' I thought, 'that a complete stranger should stop me and offer me a drink.' We went to a pleasant pub. 'What would you like to drink?' he asked.

'Half a beer, please.'

My conversation in those days must have been hard work, but undaunted he pressed on. 'And where do you come from?'

'The West Indies,' I replied. Not true – but I suppose I wanted to impress.

He wasn't impressed. 'But you have a pronounced Yorkshire accent!' he pointed out.

'Oh no,' I insisted. 'I'm from the West Indies.' He realised he had taken on a thoroughly tiresome youth and departed.

My first Royal Navy posting was to the Far East. Skins became darker as we travelled south but I felt no more at home. I was travelling aboard a liner. We crossed the Bay of Biscay, rounded Spain, and made our first port of call at Gibraltar. It was the first time I had been outside the UK and I was fascinated to see not only a few blacks but many North Africans with brown skins. Our next stop was Malta; then came the Suez Canal. Here of course there were many black bodies to be seen and I noted that they were always subservient, following our ship through the Canal in their little boats, diving for coins, selling items that could be bought quite cheaply, even looking for scraps of food. The poverty shocked me. I could not believe that people knew such poverty. Then we reached India, and there everything was infinitely worse.

We landed in Bombay. The dreadful state of some of the Indians on the streets was something I will never forget. There were children who were deliberately maimed to make them more plausible beggars. Hundreds of people, whole families, slept on the streets at night, and rats crawled over their bodies. I have never seen such depravity. It was many years before I became aware of the caste system and the so-called Untouchables, but already I had an intense if untutored interest in, and horror of, prejudice and discrimination of any sort.

Strangely, very much later in life, when I was living in Chesterfield, my closest friend was an Indian, Dr Anand Bhoomkar, a consultant physician, who died in 1991. Our friendship was warm and close, and I miss him all the time, yet we were poles apart in every respect – personality, background, disposition. There was so much to divide us. I despise the caste system of his country, India. I could never have attained my present social mobility had I been born there, for surely I would have been an Untouchable. Anand was a Brahmin and a doctor; he was also a poet and an intellectual. He had never experienced deprivation or want; yet he came from a country where the conditions of the poor had horrified me when I saw them as a naval stoker.

Anand and I used to discuss this. I could never accept his complacency about the poverty of India; yet could never make my point clearly. I was verbose but not articulate, the same impasse I used to reach when I tried to describe factory life to my teacher colleagues. Yet somehow, despite our innumerable differences, Anand and I were exceptionally close.

After Bombay, the next port of call was Colombo, capital of what was then called Ceylon. I visited a tea plantation high in the mountains above the low-lying clouds. It is difficult to imagine that such a beautiful island and such an apparently peace-loving people would be torn by civil strife and tribal conflict in my middle age. Yet the seeds of dispute were already there, the situation aggravated by the low standard of living of those working in the tea plantations.

In Singapore, I saw what I thought were the most beautiful women anywhere in the world. Over the years, mixed marriages between a variety of races had produced a complete colour range from white to black via khaki and amber. So there could be no problems there caused by skin pigmentation, I realised, which was reassuring. And so, apart from my naval uniform, I felt quite at ease. Yet though there was no colour prejudice, there was still that oriental division between the very rich and the very poor, which was food for thought. Skin colour is important, I was learning, but so are economics.

It was that strange time, immediately after the war. During the Indonesians' struggle for independence from the Dutch, following the Japanese surrender, I was posted to a landing craft and crossed the Malacca Straits from Singapore to Sumatra, presumably to help protect the principal harbour of Medan. Besides Sumatra we visited ports in Burma, Malaysia, and, in India, Bombay and Madras, ports where prostitution was necessary just to feed and clothe the children. The stench was often unbearable, and at night the beggars and the vermin shared the stinking streets. The British servicemen referred to these natives as 'wogs', and I was a wog too in their eyes.

My shipmates' sense of superiority was misplaced but not surprising. It was almost indoctrinated among certain sectors of British society that white Englishmen of whatever class or income bracket were superior to those whom Kipling called 'lesser breeds without the law'. What the British servicemen saw on their travels often endorsed what they believed. Nor was I in any position to test my companions' prejudices. With my lack of formal education, social graces and self-assurance, I could do little to prove that non-whites and whites were equal in the sight of God. Indeed, my naval adventure, rather than making a man of me as I had promised myself it would, reinforced and perpetuated my chronic inferiority complex. I returned to civilian life wallowing in self-doubt. And then something happened which transformed my life.

PART 2

RUNNING

Chapter 2

In 1947, after my naval service, I returned to Leeds, having nowhere better to go, and found employment at the Yorkshire Copper Works in Hunslet as a lorry driver's mate. Each day eight loads of coke had to be moved from the local railway goods yards to the factory. Huge forks were used to unload the waggons entirely by hand.

My driver, Harry, was a bantam but aggressive. We were physically like David and Goliath, but he dominated me with his cunning and arrogance. In his own way he enjoyed life to the full, exploiting every situation to his own advantage. Fags, booze, blondes and boobs fed his appetite; he seemed to be totally unrestrained in his sexual activity. He was continually telling me what a wonderful worker I was; he was so impressed with my workrate he became quite ecstatic, sitting snug in his cab, especially during storms of torrential rain, seeing how fast I could load the lorry with coke. It took about six months for my retarded brain to catch up on his crafty strategy.

After a short while Harry started giving me bags of copper to take to a local scrap dealer, maybe £3 or £4 worth, and he would give me five shillings (25p) for my trouble. He was always talking about his various sensual pleasures as we drove the streets, about the women he spotted, and their tits, arses and crutches. In fact, his anatomically crude remarks and my own reflections on my naval adventures made this mind-numbing job far more tolerable than anything I had known before my nautical life.

Then one day the works manager called me into his office and told me that I had been used as a decoy for Harry's underhand activities of stealing and selling company property! However, he said that on this occasion he would let me off with a warning.

Anyway, that year at Kirkstall Forge and all that shovelling of coke for Harry was probably how my body was prepared for what lay ahead when out of the blue, in 1948, I was asked to play for the firm in an annual Rugby League works tournament in Bramley. The firm's team was weak and I was 6 foot and 14 stone; and rather than be labelled a coward, I agreed. I had never played the game before and I cannot believe I had much natural talent. But what I brought to the occasion, in abundance, was enthusiasm.

Enthusiasm has always been my greatest ally, and it is to my enthusiasm that I owe what successes I have enjoyed in my life. At times my enthusiasm seems almost inexhaustible, constantly moving me forward, sweeping into almost every department of my life, my chosen occupation, my home and my recreation. Enthusiasm was also enough, apparently, to excite the interest of Rugby League scouts – from Hunslet, Dewsbury and Bramley – who always made a point of watching the matches in that works competition.

In those first games I played, ignorant of the rules, I received just two instructions: first, don't pass the ball forward, and, second, don't kick it. Armed with this valuable advice, I was keen to begin. Keeping close to my forwards in the scrums, I tried to tackle any opponent who had the ball. I ran, and ran, and ran. I never stopped running. At times I had no idea where or why I was running. After my second game, a Hunslet scout came up to me and said how impressed he had been by my tackling and by my non-stop running. 'Where doz tha' git all tha' bloody energy fra'? Tha' lakes a reet gud game!'

To my astonishment Hunslet offered me a contract and I signed for them in 1948 for the huge sum of £250. I felt like a millionaire. I began my professional career in the reserve or A team whose principal function is to develop budding newcomers like myself – though surely no one had ever been quite as raw as I was – and to give ageing players a game before they retired. My first match was against Castleford A.

Castleford had an ageing prop forward in their team with rolled up sleeves, bulging muscles, missing teeth, broken nose and cauliflower ears. When he rolled up his sleeves he looked like Popeye after a car smash. He lumbered his 17 stone over to me, glared, and said, 'If you touch that so-and-so ball, I'll break your so-and-so neck.' I wanted to return that £250 without a second's delay. Still, after the game, Popeye came up to me again (both sides used the same bath) and said, 'That's the Castleford way of saying "Welcome to the game" – I've never seen you before but you've done all right!'

Becoming a professional Rugby League player in the Hunslet A team was like entering a dream-world as exhilarating as falling in love. There may have been little more than 500 to 600 spectators at our home matches but it was a totally new experience for me to be watched by so many. Though in my very first year, in December 1948, I fractured the tibia in my left leg, and was out of action for several months, I really enjoyed the game, began to acquire some skills, played well enough in an excellent team to win the A team champion-ship, and even made ten appearances in the first team before I was injured.

When I was promoted to the first team I could hardly cope with my excitement and the highly charged atmosphere of the game. The speed and skill of the players left little time for thought. Most of the action is instinctive, a split-second's hesitation earns a tackle like a sledgehammer's blow. I soon realised that at first-team level the physical punishment in every game is ferociously demanding; and total com-mitment was needed simply to keep one's place in the side.

It took me several games to learn other facts of my new professional sporting life. Once I was supporting my second-row partner, who had made a break with only one man to beat for the try-line some ten metres away. I called for the ball; he looked at me but ran on to try to beat his one remaining opponent but was tackled in possession. After the match, I realised that he was playing for his place in the team and in that context he saw me as a rival. Players can be cynical when there is keen rivalry for places in the side.

Off the field it was a sad period for me. The frustration of my broken leg was bad enough, but that winter was bitterly cold. The snow drifted on the streets and then froze. It was bad enough to be able-bodied in such weather; for me, on my crutches, it was intolerable. And then, in the midst of that awful winter, in January 1949, my mother was taken to hospital. I went to see her. I didn't know she had cancer but when I saw this fine woman rapidly become a skeleton, it was clear that she was dying. I have never felt so abandoned, so desolate. My stepfather and I took turns to visit her, which meant we were rarely at home at the same time. The house was cold and empty and so was I. Poor Edwin: my mother's death seemed to rob him of any desire to live. He lost all interest in the business and eventually sold it and went to live nearby with his sister, Anne.

My leg recovered but my mother's death seemed to take with it my enthusiasm for the professional game. I felt I had to get away from Leeds, and decided to try my hand as a kitchen help in a London hotel. I tramped the London streets looking for jobs in various hotels but in vain. My feet were swollen and painful; I was exhausted, unwashed and hungry. I slept on a bench in Hyde Park and next morning hitchhiked home. I felt physically, mentally and spiritually bankrupt but at least I could cope with Leeds again. For a while I worked for my stepfather in his bakery until I found a new job with Bison Concrete, on the periphery of Hunslet, in the close season of 1949 and started rugby training again. During the 1949–50 season, I was a member of the Hunslet A team which won the Yorkshire Cup as well as playing some more games for the first team.

My new job at Bison Concrete consisted of wheeling barrow loads of concrete into moulds for making prestressed concrete slabs for various buildings around the country. The thought of going back to the Yorkshire Copper Works filled me with apprehension. I was grateful for the let-off I had been given by the works manager but wanted to be nowhere near the place where, all unwittingly, I had broken the law.

Richard Hoggart, who was born in Hunslet, describes in *The Uses of Literacy* the cobbled streets and washing-lines between the terraces which I remember only too well. His book conveys vividly the poverty of Hunslet, a poverty which was not only economic but also a poverty of culture and opportunity. I think it is fair to say that the rugby club was Hunslet's proudest claim to fame.

Across the city, at Headingley, is another Rugby League club, Leeds. Headingley is on the posh (north) side of Leeds; Hunslet, to the south, over Leeds Bridge, which crosses the river Aire, was really pretty rough. Hunslet people have a distinct accent and dialect, and in the 1950s a muffler, flat cloth cap and a boiler suit was the typical dress when players came for training. However, everyone seemed to enjoy a few pints of beer at the weekend and greyhound racing was, and still is, a popular leisure pursuit.

I don't suppose I was a typical Rugby League player. My institutional upbringing in an orphanage had left its mark on me. By nature I am a pacifist; I don't swear; I don't smoke; at that period of my life I drank no alcohol. Perhaps my most striking characteristic though, apart from my colour, was a fear of females. These attributes, combined with my christian names of Theodore Cecil, meant that some of the players thought I must be gay, which is not a reputation anyone would want in professional rugby. Yet though they were a tough bunch, those players, I shall be indebted to them for the rest of my life. They were hard but courageous and generous too. Because they knew I always gave my best on the field, they looked after me. A player can be easily hurt if the opposition is playing flat out and there is a collision between an opponent's fist and your face, but my team-mates always protected me from unfair play. In fact, I think the opposition eventually learned to leave me alone, knowing that twelve of my mates would retaliate if I went down. It gave me a hugely comforting feeling.

As the players befriended and defended me, I started to gain in confidence. Sometimes, after I had established myself in the first team, fans asked for my autograph. But all I could do was to print my name – which was embarrassing to say the least. So, as I started to try to better myself, my first priority was to improve my handwriting. My next was to learn to make casual conversation and, though these may seem pretty elementary skills for the average person, they were far from straightforward for me.

All the travelling to away matches helped to expand my horizons. Ever since my time in the navy, travel has played a big part in my life, but I only started to recognise its importance for me on those coach trips with the Hunslet team around Yorkshire, Lancashire and Cumbria. I also began to see how desultory my life had been before I started to play professional rugby. The game provided an escape-route to a happier, brighter and more exciting world. But if I lived better than I had done, I could not fail to notice that the life-style of the club's directors was very different. They and their wives seemed so much more sophisticated than the players. I found myself increasingly aware of social differences. Some people I encountered had effortless charm, while somehow I seemed to lack dignity. Because I was a loner I was also a dreamer, but though I dreamed of becoming well educated and self-assured, I hadn't the first idea of how to go about it.

However, my first priority clearly was to improve my game and gradually I acquired sufficient skills to support my extraordinary God-given energy. After Hunslet had beaten St Helens 8–2 in the 1949–50 season, in one of my appearances for the first team, the *Daily Herald* wrote:

Thompson impressed with his pace, speed on the ball and dogged persistence. He works his way through the game with an enthusiasm and stamina unequalled anywhere else in the Hunslet side and at the final whistle he is usually going as hard as he was at the start. He has now pretty well established himself in the second row of the pack: Hunslet has a rule that a player gets his blazer after fifteen games in the first team and this was the darkie's fifteenth.

After Hunslet had beaten Castleford 17–8 at Wheldon Road in the following season, when I had won a more or less permanent place in the side, this match report appeared:

The Parksiders are still far from perfect but they were given a wonderful lead by their pack on this occasion. It is a long time since I saw such a wholehearted forward display as that given by their second-row man Theodore Cecil Thompson. His liveliness had to be seen to be believed and he was well backed up by his second-row partner, Ted Carroll. Thompson scored an excellent solo try which really put Hunslet on the winning path.

After the game I was given a standing ovation by the 9,000 crowd, which moved me deeply, particularly as it was on foreign soil. I felt as if I had won an Olympic gold and imagined myself in the centre of a delirious crowd in a huge amphitheatre somewhere. But I was still only at Wheldon Road, Castleford with the colliery pit-tips in the background. Later that season, after we had beaten Bradford Northern 14-10, the Hunslet crowd went wild, according to the local paper, 'celebrating a great try by Thompson. From a play-the-ball forty yards out, Thompson shook off two tackles, beat Phillips, the full-back, and dived over for a brilliant solo try.'

So I suppose I was beginning to make my mark on the game.

Rugby League is still seen by many people in this country as a bit of north of England eccentricity. They seem to think it belongs with fish and chip shops, tripe and onions, cloth caps, slag heaps, textile mills and chimney stacks, black pudding and brass bands, as a sort of Rugby Union game adapted to the primitive needs of northern peasants.

It was bad enough to be black. Now I found, if I told anyone I played Rugby League, that I had acquired yet another label. How much lower down the social scale could one go than be seen as a black, uneducated, Rugby League player who was also an unskilled, manual labourer? I have to say that rugby never came naturally to me; for example, I found that passing a ball any distance was practically impossible. However, my supreme fitness gave me immense power on the field. If we kicked off, as the ball was propelled diagonally towards the opposing forwards, I would race to wherever I thought it would drop and then leap to catch it before it could get within reach of the receiver. Such feats captured attention and won ovations and such comments as, 'Who is that black bugger always leaping for the ball?'

It was a recognised ploy for full-backs to try to outkick their opposite number or force a handling error or find touch and thus gain an important territorial advantage. An attacking full-back would often try to set up an attack out of defence, especially if he had a devastating side-step. Once an opposing full-back had put me onside, I would keep him in my sights and bring him crashing to the ground with a spectacular diving tackle. Today, Wigan and a number of other clubs play this game when the sixth tackle is announced, with a deep kick, and their superbly fit forwards crowd out the opposing full-back.

Few forwards in the game had the fitness first to do the required running and then to make a remarkable leap. Tackling was my great strength. Often I became aware, as Eddie Waring, the late BBC Rugby League commentator, once pointed out, that some of my team-mates would let me do more than my share of tackling, leaving them fresh to shine in attack. However, all my antics could not compensate me for my lack of natural talent. I could not be compared with the great stars of the game. I played more games with Brian Edgar (of whom more later) than any other second-row partner; and at Hunslet another contemporary was Geoff Gunney, on a par with Edgar but a different type of player. Among other brilliant forwards of my time were Johnny Whiteley of Hull, Rocky Turner of Wakefield Trinity and Oldham, Vince Karalius (the 'wild bull of the Pampas') of St Helens, and Brian Shaw of Hunslet and Leeds, all streets ahead of me in skill. So I had to fight for media attention, realising that I had to make things happen on the field, largely by strength and fitness, or life would pass me by.

Training, compared to today's sophisticated activities, was really pretty primitive. In my day little attention was paid to the development of playing skills. Training took place on two nights a week and consisted simply of a few laps of the pitch to warm up, a little sprint-training, maybe a series of boring exercises, scrum practice for the forwards and passing movements for the backs, with a game of touch-and-pass to finish off. That was the full extent of match practice. No one taught me the basic skills of the game or explained team tactics and strategy or even kept me up to date with changes in the rules! These important elements had to be picked up in rudimentary form by watching and copying. The rest of my play, and indeed the skills of most of my contemporaries, was largely instinctive. So with a minimum of experience and no teaching, I had little to offer compared to my contemporaries.

However, thanks to Eddie Waring, the game in the early 1950s was at last earning some wider recognition. And as Eddie also had a weekly column in the Sunday press, my name began to be known to a wider public. In 1951–52 I had won a permanent place in the first team and had become a sort of minor Hunslet hero. Eddie was fascinated with my exuberant style of play and did his best to get me selected for Great Britain in the first Test against New Zealand in October 1951, little more than four years after my first stumbling match for the Hunslet works team. Some rugby writers are able to make a player seem sensational, and sometimes selectors bow to that pressure. Eddie wrote, 'If Cec Thompson is not chosen for the Great Britain squad (to face New Zealand), the selectors must be racists.' He also gave me excellent press reports for many weeks before and after that startling statement. Admittedly I had been in good form and was duly selected.

That first Test was at the Odsal Stadium, Bradford, with its capacity at the time of 100,000. To put on that red, white and blue jersey was a tremendous moment. As each player's name was called, he peeled from the line to receive the crowd's applause, and it was great to hear my name blared over the tannoy: 'Cec Thompson'. I had been proud to serve my country in the navy but to represent Great Britain at sport left me elated.

There must have been plenty of Hunslet supporters in the crowd because I got a great ovation. I played well, but not quite to the extent of this press report, a glowing hyperbole by Alfred Drewry in the *Yorkshire Post*:

> It's queer how blind people can be to facts. I had only seen Thompson once before the Test, and was struck by the natural way he seemed to fit in with Rugby League style. 'Oh, he's all right,' said a very good judge of Yorkshire players, 'but he isn't top-class.'
>
> Now if there was a forward on the Great Britain side who looked top-class in the Test, where Thompson came to judgement, it was the Hunslet living bronze. His poise, his grace, his swerve, and lithe easy action were a delight to see. He reminded me for all the world of those old bronze figures that were once all the go for mantel decoration. An athlete poised with one foot on a ball, needing only wings to be too good for this earth.

Maybe that was going over the top a bit, but at least I performed sufficiently well to be selected to play in the second Test at Swinton and thus, having being picked twice, became the proud possessor of an international cap.

This is what the *Daily Herald* had to say about my first unforgettable international, which Great Britain won 21–15. It was headlined HUNSLET'S 'DARKIE' ONE OF BRITAIN'S HEROES.

> Cheers for 'unknowns' Greenall and 'Darkie' Thompson who, playing in their first honours match of any kind, were unsurpassed by colleagues or rivals.
>
> Great Britain started in fine style. Wilson and Cracknell were sent flying down their respective wings to score as a result of smart passing by the British centres. It was at this point that our lads looked like running up a cricket score for the New Zealand defence was several times extended by deep thrusts on the part of Williams, Ward and Thompson. Then for some reason the New Zealanders were galvanised into action while at the same

time Britain began to fold. An early 8-points lead did not deter the Kiwis and they began to show their immense power in the forwards. Atkinson and McLennan were held inches from the line before Johnson hurled himself over for a try. New Zealand continued their powerhouse tactics in the second half and when Great Britain did try to get the ball moving they were inevitably stopped by close marking.

Proof was shown of what could have been done had the ball reached the Kiwis' threequarters when Robertson neatly skipped through for a fine try. Then came the British revival, well led by Ernest Ward. First Greenall and then Wilson (twice) penetrated the Kiwis' defence. A late rally by New Zealand produced a try by Eastlake which White goaled. Well fought New Zealand! More of this type of play will ensure the tour's success.

Great Britain: Cunliffe (Wigan); Cracknell (Huddersfield), Greenall (St Helens), Ward (Bradford Northern), Wilson (Workington Town); Williams (Leeds), Burnell (Hunslet); Gee (Wigan), McKeating (Workington Town), Gwyther (Belle Vue Rangers), Thompson (Hunslet), Ryan (Warrington), Blan (Wigan).

New Zealand: White; Baxter, M. Robertson, Hough, Haig; Menzies, Eastlake; Johnson, Davidson, McLennan, McBride, Mulcare, Atkinson.

My second Test was the first ever to be played in front of a TV camera. It was a tremendous thrill-a-minute match in which the lead was constantly changing. Eventually Great Britain won by the narrowest margin, 20–19, when a Kiwi victory seemed certain. Most felt before the game that the New Zealand pack would prove too much for us but the reverse was true. Jimmy Ledgard had a good game at full-back and it was fortunate for Great Britain that he kicked well that day while his opposite number, White, was off form. Williams, playing his

first game as Britain's captain, led the side well, his contribution good
enough to single him out as Britain's man-of-the-match.

The New Zealanders were unfortunate to lose and the fact that they
scored five tries to Britain's four was a fair reflection of the run of
play, though Britain's fighting spirit carried them through in the end.
First Cracknell, Burnell and Williams paved the way for Traill to score
under the posts and then Ward cut through, a piece of perfect centre
play which gave Wilson a try on a plate.

The teams that day were:

Great Britain: Ledgard (Leigh); Cracknell (Huddersfield), Greenall
(St Helens), Ward (Bradford Northern), Wilson (Workington
Town); Williams (Leeds), Burnell (Hunslet); Gee (Wigan),
McKeating (Workington Town), Prescott (St Helens), Thompson
(Hunslet), Blan (Wigan), Traill (Bradford Northern).

New Zealand: White; B. Robertson, Baxter, M. Robertson, For-
rest; Eastlake, Barchard; Johnson, Davidson, McLennan, McBride,
Mulcare, Atkinson.

I was the first black player to play for Great Britain at Rugby League.
Both Tests, and so the series, had been won. Then the team was
changed to give new players the chance to shine in the third and final
Test, and I stood down. In the same season I was selected for the
Yorkshire squad, was chosen to travel with the England side to play
France, played for the British Empire team against Wales at Llanelli
and to crown a great year I toured France with my club, Hunslet.

However, despite my successes on the field of play, and some glowing
press reports, I continued to feel terribly insecure as a person. In every
new environment I entered I was always the object of much teasing
and still would never speak unless spoken to. Today, I am rather
talkative and my present associates cannot believe that I was once so
shy and self-effacing. And my wife was incredulous when my old
team-mates first told her what an introvert I used to be.

Those visits to France with England and then with Hunslet will always remain vivid in my memory. It was the first time I had flown in a plane; in the south of France we were welcomed like royalty. I remember realising that here I was, a black boy from the slums of Leeds, a factory labourer, flying from Ringway airport to represent my club – but I can't remember if the thought was sobering or intoxicating. Everything was done in great style. A brass band greeted us when we landed at Toulouse airport, and a champagne reception was held in our honour.

In a normal season at home we played representative teams and attended receptions, but now we were the tourists, and life off the field began to assume a special importance. It was Paris – needless to say – which really stirred my imagination. After our last match there we wandered round the Pigalle district to inspect the various nightclubs. Most of the players had more experience of life than I had, so I merely tagged along to see the nude shows, not normally being a drinker. Nevertheless I was persuaded to have a drink or two and the night became more and more convivial.

In Paris I was truly like a duck out of water. I found it difficult to believe that people could live such glittering lives as some of those I saw there. What made it worse for me was that I realised that they were behaving quite naturally whereas I had always to watch what others did before I could order or eat or drink in a restaurant. My experiences since signing for Hunslet had taught me a lot but they had not taught me enough. How could those middle- and upper-class people I saw in the nightclubs and restaurants be at ease in those luxurious surroundings while I felt so absolutely inadequate? And what a culture shock it was to return from that grand hotel in a fashionable area of Paris to my job as a lorry driver's mate in Hunslet.

As my career with Hunslet developed, I became a valued and apparently irreplaceable member of the side. One newspaper report had this to say:

Thompson, whose previous appearances in the first team were

always marked by spirit, has in his recent matches shown considerable added polish in his play and has lost nothing of his zeal. He has become an invaluable member of the team and it is a very long time since I saw such a wholehearted display as that given by Theodore Cecil Thompson.

In a drawn match against Leeds, I was adjudged the star: 'No one was as much in the picture as T. C. Thompson, whose dash and effectiveness made him the leading forward on either side.'

Most flattering of all, Gus Risman, the former Great Britain captain, soon to sign me for Workington Town, had this to say in his regular newspaper column: 'The playing ability of Boston and Thompson would be invaluable on the forthcoming tour to Australia. Selectors, please forget any prejudice about colour . . .'

One effect of my new international status was that locally I was being accorded a sort of stardom. I was attracting the attention of the Hunslet fans, and some of them were attractive women. Girls had never been part of my life: my sexual desire was strong, but my shyness stronger. But now I was in a situation when it was the women who were making the running. In particular, there was a startling brunette who idolised me. She pursued me relentlessly and soon I was bowled over. Barbara was the first girlfriend I had ever had, and as so often seems to happen in cases such as this things developed far too fast. Within a few months we were engaged; in eighteen months we were married, with the Hunslet team as a guard of honour – though I cannot imagine whose honour they were meant to guard.

In those days it was rare to see a black person, never mind a black-white couple linking arms, so I used to walk whenever possible along the back streets to avoid the main roads. I felt guilty, as though I was doing wrong; it was as if I was breaking the apartheid laws of South Africa, but here I was, an Englishman in England. I have often wondered how my father must have felt when he was courting my mother in rural County Durham. In me this sensation of trespassing developed into a desire to be inconspicuous. Like a fox being chased in the countryside by hounds, I imagined I had to be wily in order to survive.

Barbara had been dazzled by my public acclaim, and I had been dazzled by her looks. I am afraid it did not take us long to realise that our personalities were incompatible. We were living in Hunslet with her parents – a shaky foundation for a lasting relationship at the best of times – in a house about ten minutes walk from the ground at Parkside. The in-laws were fine people, but there were constant disagreements between Barbara and me, and these became increasingly difficult. I asked Barbara what she thought of the idea of me transferring to another club, away from West Yorkshire. I suggested that a place of our own, new surroundings, and a change of club might bring about a more harmonious relationship, and Barbara agreed. I told the press and my club that I wished to move for personal reasons, which was true, and discovered that, after five years as a raw recruit, initially signed for £250, my value had increased to £2,500.

Sport can be unpredictable. People in the public eye expend a lot of nervous as well as muscular energy as they pursue their particular talents. It is impossible to predict what your performance will be like in any match: sometimes you give of your best and are a complete failure; at other times everything turns up trumps. I had played against Gus Risman's team, Workington Town, both home and away within four weeks, and had had two brilliant games. Gus wrote a column in the Sunday press in which he claimed that I was the best forward he had played against that season and he started to pursue me the moment my name appeared on the transfer list.

So at the end of the 1952–53 season I said goodbye to Hunslet after five memorable years, with two Test appearances, a number of representative matches under my belt and some flattering press reports. I did not play Test rugby again though I nearly scraped into the Great Britain touring side to Australia in 1958. For all Eddie Waring's enthusiasm, and my own strength and fitness, I was just not good enough for international rugby. But I like to think that I scaled some pretty lofty heights in the years to come at Workington.

Chapter 3

The north-west coast of Cumbria embraces the industrial towns of Whitehaven, Workington and Maryport: not exactly the most picturesque parts of the county. Inland, however, are the beauties of the Lake District, and it was these, as much as Gus Risman, that persuaded me to join Workington. I felt immediately that I had made the right decision. Just as welcoming as the hills and lakes were the people of Cumbria, warm-hearted, hospitable and generous.

Workington Town was an impressive club at that time. Almost every member of the team was an international. For those were the days when there were not only international matches between Great Britain and Australia, Great Britain and New Zealand, and England and France, but also composite international teams embracing players from other nationalities – maybe Australians, New Zealanders and South Africans – who were playing in the English league. Though Workington was a relatively small community, we regularly attracted gates of 15,000 to our home games.

Everything in life suddenly seemed much easier. One day, just before my transfer, I was called into the office at Bison Concrete to find several elegantly groomed gentlemen with cultured voices seated round a large table. A voice asked me to sit down. I said, 'I feel better standing, thank you.' I thought, 'What have I done wrong?' I was shaking a little.

Another voice said, 'We've heard from various sources that you are considered a celebrity with the local rugby team. As representatives of the company we would like to promote you to be an inspector.' From that day I began inspecting the quality of my colleagues' work and came to realise that I could do it quite well. I discovered that I had an innate talent for helping others to improve their work, a talent which much later I proved again during my teaching career.

To some extent this promotion was in recognition of my newly won international status in Rugby League. My new club could not find me a job to equal what Bison Concrete had given me but they paid me what I had been paid before anyway, on top of my playing wages. This gave me a degree of financial security. I found myself happier in Cumbria than I had ever been before. It was partly the environment. I was enraptured by the Lake District, as I still am today. But there was more to my happiness than that. I was at last beginning to feel that I just might be worth something in the world. Certainly my style of living had blossomed beyond my wildest hopes. I had bought a car, and thereby fulfilled a dream I had had since the days of the Tynemouth orphanage. Though most of my team-mates had cars and would not have regarded my acquisition as anything special, to me it felt like real achievement. My social life changed remarkably. Business people began inviting me to their clubs. I was rubbing shoulders with middle-class people: a new world was at my feet.

In the Workington team were five Australians who brought a cosmopolitan flavour to the club. Australians seem often larger than life, and these five were no exception. Their outlook fascinated me and I found their liveliness and self-assurance illuminating. Of course it was all a bit unreal really: this environment that glittered so brightly for me was still just a rural backwater. But how wonderful was the landscape and how stimulating were most of the people I met and worked with.

As my horizons expanded and life became more interesting, success on the field led to successes in other directions. Barbara told me how marvellous the place was, and how pleased she was that we had made the move: 'I am much happier now that we have a home of our own', she said. So for a time we were fairly content. And it certainly makes a difference to a player's form when he has a stable life at home, though I still had to prove myself as a player with Workington. I felt as though

I was in a glass bowl now that I was away from Leeds with its population of over half a million. If I had been conspicuous in the West Riding, I was like a Martian in Cumbria. But a very popular Martian: eyes were always on me on and off the field.

Starting to play professional rugby with no previous experience of the game had been asking a lot of myself. Most players develop their skills from childhood: I had had to pick up knowledge of the game as I went along. My tactical skills were severely limited and I had had to use all my native wit to hide my inexperience. My biggest ally was fitness. If I were fast enough and strong enough I believed I would survive, and survival has always been my first priority.

Now at Workington my game really began to blossom. I was fit and my fitness nearly always got me into the right place to support a break, for example, which – because of the quality of my team-mates – meant that I scored quite a few tries. This in turn made me popular with the fans. Hundreds would come to see us training at the beginning of the season and I came to realise how exhilarating it can be to be part of a successful team, among talented players and with such whole-heartedly enthusiastic supporters. But above all else, in those early days at Workington, it was Gus Risman who was the inspiration.

Gus, at full-back, was magnificent; a handsome and athletically built 6-footer, his presence had a tremendous influence on me because he always led by example. Indeed, Gus is my ideal of what a professional games player should be, intelligent, dignified and with no nonsense about him. He would have a few halves of beer with the team, but would never be the worse for alcohol. He and his wife Ethel were extremely hospitable and arranged many happy parties for the team and our wives or girlfriends at their home in Cockermouth.

I remembered those games against Gus when I was still at Hunslet. Once, after we had narrowly defeated Workington, he came over to me. 'You're a newcomer to the game, aren't you?' he asked.

'This is my third season, but I suffered a broken leg in my first,' I replied.

'I was very impressed,' said Gus. 'Keep it up.'

'Thank you,' I answered. 'I'll try.' I felt elevated; I felt as if God had spoken to me.

Towards the end of the same season Hunslet had played Workington again, at Workington, and with two minutes to go Hunslet were one point behind Town. I broke clear of the opposition and raced to within fifteen yards of the try-line, with only Gus at full-back to beat. I drew Gus and passed the ball to Laurie Gant in support. Gus was a difficult player to beat and I was elated, until with the line wide open and a Hunslet victory in sight, Laurie dropped the ball.

Gus's career covered twenty-five years, and he played until the age of forty-three. He toured Australia three times with the Great Britain side, the last time as captain. He won thirty-six Test and international caps, he played in three Wembley Cup finals, six winning League Championship finals and won five Lancashire League Championship winners medals. By the time I joined Workington Town at the start of the 1953–54 season, Gus was at the end of his career. A fitness fanatic, he was still a superb performer with an amazing turn of speed for his age. He must have run like a gazelle in his heyday. His outstanding contribution to the team was his work as a diplomat. Workington had been of little importance in terms of sport until Gus's arrival as player-manager, though strangely the local soccer club, with whom we then shared a ground, had an equally famous manager in Bill Shankly, who went on to win glory at Liverpool. Gus's great skill lay in assembling successful combinations of players, in building a team in other words. And he could read a game the way other men read a newspaper.

I was lucky enough to make a dream debut for Workington in a match against Dewsbury at Crown Flatt, scoring a try within ten minutes and making two others during the match. The press greeted my arrival with this report:

Workington's forwards were not only fast but clever. Gus can give himself a pat on the back for his prize close-season signing. Cecil Thompson, a £2,500 forward buy from Hunslet, scored a try within ten minutes. He and the loose forward, Billy Ivison, the big brains in a wonderful pack, struck up a brilliant understanding in no time at all and their clever construction work, featured by skilful use of the reverse pass, was a delight to watch.

Workington reached the Championship Cup final in May 1955 at the end of my first season, but lost to Barrow by 12–21. Sadly I missed the match, still nursing a knee injury sustained three months earlier in a match against Swinton which we won 22–0. My injury let Brian Edgar into the side as my replacement, thus beginning an outstanding career for a player who was already a talented junior international. As the years went by he developed into one of the finest second-row forwards in the game and for the next three years Brian and I consistently formed the second-row for Town.

Then, at the beginning of my third season with Workington, on Saturday 8 October 1955, when Sol Roper was injured, I was elected captain in his place for the two or three matches he had to miss. This was a remarkable honour and I was especially pleased by what the press had to say after my first game as skipper:

Thompson inspired a great Town rally. Persistent work in the loose by their captain and second-row forward displayed great leadership. His inspiring example was crowned by a magnificent individual try when he broke clean through the opposition, urging his men on to better things. Cecil Thompson was easily the man-of-the-match. Two of his defence-splitting runs yielded tries, and then the big forward was on hand to finish off a round of passing with a try for himself.

Another paper carried this report:

Sepia-skinned Cec Thompson, wise in the ways of field craft and master of the delayed pass, put the only polish on to this roughly hewn game. Workington had the ideas, Cec saw to that. Indeed, the Workington skipper set a fine example by his inspiring leadership.

Occasionally my speed and size won me selection on the wing, especially when a big free-scoring winger opposed us. In the first round of the Challenge Cup against Halifax, at Thrum Hall in 1956, for example, such a winger was Johnny Freeman from Tiger Bay, Cardiff. This press report pleased me no end:

Cec Thompson's try was a beauty. Freeman lost possession after being crash-tackled by Thompson and the ball was thrust into Thompson's hands by Gibson. Cec hared up the touchline, rounded Lynch and headed for Griffiths with Sol Roper in support infield. He feinted to pass inside to the half-back but carried on with a swerve to go round the full-back and touch down.

After another match, when we had beaten the League leaders, St Helens, this report appeared:

The forwards, led by Cec Thompson, blunted St Helens's power. No one could hope to stop Cec's blockbusting raids, giving a performance which he will never better. He featured in every probe and before he crashed over for a try in the dying seconds of the first half, he had dealt blow after blow at the tightly packed St Helens defence. Thompson's inspiration had swung the game in Workington's favour.

Apart from meeting Gus, another wonderful relationship which developed from my moving to Workington was with Gus's son, Bev. Bev, who was born in 1937, became almost as famous as his remarkable father, but his career illustrates some of the tensions between the two codes of rugby. Even as a schoolboy Bev played both Union as captain of Cockermouth Grammar School, and amateur Rugby League, training with Workington Town's first team. At first, Bev favoured Union.

He was made captain of England Schoolboys, went on to Manchester University where he captained both the University XV and the England Universities XV, and became a full England international while still a student. In 1959, he played stand-off for England and toured New Zealand with the British Lions, and he won his Bachelor of Science Honours degree in Geology. For once the son of a famous father was doing famously.

Unfortunately for Bev, however, his Union career coincided with that of Richard Sharp, a truly brilliant fly-half. In 1960 Bev lost his England place to his dazzling rival: it seemed to be no more than a temporary hiccup in his career for he spent the year at Loughborough College, ending it not only with a postgraduate diploma in physical education, but also with a recall to the international scene. He played two games at stand-off against Wales and the touring Springboks, and a couple more at centre against France and Ireland. But Sharp was always going to be the selectors' first choice, and when Bev was omitted from the final match against Scotland, he decided to turn professional.

Bev signed for Leigh in March 1961 but his moments of greatest glory came when, almost five years later, he joined Leeds. He and the Headingley club were perfectly suited, and Bev, fielding a variety of kicks with unruffled serenity, tackling soundly, kicking with shrewd tactical precision, and gliding unhurriedly into attack to feed the men up front with masterly timing, was playing magnificent rugby. As for goalkicking, twice he came within a whisker of beating Lewis Jones's record-breaking tally of 166: in 1966–67 he landed 163 goals and two years later 165.

Sadly, his playing career was terminated abruptly by a knee injury, sustained against Warrington at Wilderspool in February 1970. After this Bev headed south, lecturing in physical education and sport; for a number of years he became a fitness consultant to the national tennis squad, and wrote his well known books, *Fit for Rugby* and *Fit for Tennis*. He has also become the Rugby Football League's co-ordinator of the fast-expanding Student Rugby League. The game's image is safe in his hands. Indeed, it seems to me that Gus and Bev Risman, true sportsmen both, are synonymous with all that is best in Rugby League. Nor did the next generation of Rismans do so badly for themselves. Two of Bev's three sons, John and Mike, won rugby Blues, John for both Union and League at Oxford and Mike for Union at Cambridge.

Besides the Rismans, another who befriended me at Workington was Tom Mitchell, who throughout my playing career in Cumbria was a constant source of encouragement to me. Though we see little of each other now, for a significant part of my life Tom was a true friend. He was at that time a director, later chairman, of Workington Town Rugby League club, and is today a senior member of the RFL Council in its centenary year. A graduate of Durham University and a liberal-conservative by temperament, Tom owned huge acres of agricultural land in the north and by cultivating his land and his income with good sense and imagination had made himself into a millionaire. He was someone I looked up to and my relationship with him grew into something special.

Tom's friendship gave me immense confidence in myself. It was most unusual for a club director to join the players in pre-season training. But from the moment he and I met, Tom would compete with me on the track and over the fells. In July a bus would take the team squad to some remote setting. A route would be explained to us. We would have to run over a mountainous area, some ten to twelve miles, to a selected hotel for a meal. I can boast truthfully of having exceptional stamina and was invariably the lead runner on those occasions. But Tom would run almost the whole way with me stride by stride. I admired his tenacity enormously.

One summer, years later, my family and I were invited to go on holiday for two weeks to a medieval castle in Malta which belonged to Tom. He arrived in Malta as well, from I don't know where, and stayed with us for two days. Also staying in the castle was a young man, John Burke, just twenty-one, with his wife. Sadly, John was paralysed from the waist down from a rugby injury sustained at Workington. He was a bubbling conversationalist, always bursting with happiness. Before his injury he had had an outstanding career ahead of him and he loved talking about rugby. Tom had organised a testimonial for John which brought in sufficient money to build an all-purpose bungalow to provide for many of John's needs. At the time of our visit, John and his wife had been in Malta for three weeks and Tom had even modified the grounds of the castle so that John could be wheeled around easily. It was understood that he could always stay as Tom's guest whenever he wanted and that all expenses would always be met by Tom.

If Gus Risman was the cream of the Workington team, the other players were hardly less impressive. They were all vibrant personalities, as entertaining off the field as on, and maybe it was catching, for I found my own personality and confidence developing. That first season under Gus was a positive turning point in my life.

Perhaps the most flamboyant characters were two Australians, the late Johnny Mudge and Tony Paskins. Mudge and I were second-row partners. Mudge really was an aristocrat among forwards, stimulating to play alongside and another who led by example. He was an inspiration to me and to the rest of the forwards, and we never had a wrong word between us.

In my day Great Britain invariably beat the Australians, though nowadays of course the Aussies stand supreme and have dominated world Rugby League for twenty years, becoming altogether more professional than their British counterparts. Perhaps the first signs of this future domination were showing even in those days: certainly I was tremendously impressed by them and admired enormously their play and their assurance on the field and off. And then one day, on the team bus, Paskins referred to me as an Uncle Tom.

I could not get to sleep that night. I lay awake thinking. Was that what people really thought of me, that I was an Uncle Tom, a black man trying to ape the white man's ways? It was not how I saw myself. While it was true that I always tried to keep the peace, preferring not to react to abuse, and for that reason might have been thought of as subservient, I couldn't see how I could be an Uncle Tom. After all, I wasn't copying the English; I *was* English, both by culture and upbringing. Almost everyone I had ever spoken to was white: I had no other model. And anyway, I was English in other respects too. I paid my taxes; I had served in my country's forces; and would have fought for my country, too, shoulder to shoulder with my fellow countrymen, had I been a year or two older. If I was different from my team mates, the difference came from a deprived childhood and an inadequate education, not from the colour of my skin. I knew all that, yet said nothing, then or at any time, to Paskins. I had the passion but I did not have the words.

Tony Paskins had everything going for him. An Apollo-like figure, he was handsome, blond, blue-eyed; he was also articulate, sophisticated, a highly talented Rugby League centre, and a real ladies' man. He had been brought from the other side of the world for his playing skills, and had become a local hero. But he had an Achilles heel: insensitivity, even arrogance.

I have had dear and close friends in Australia, especially Johnny Mudge. I have always tried to avoid stereotyping other people: I have suffered enough from prejudice myself. But Paskins's stupid comment hurt me deeply, and since then I have always felt a little nervous when in the company of Australians. They seem too self-assured. I admire their lack of snobbishness, but at the same time I cannot forget their treatment of the Aborigines, nor the sort of insensitive remark that Paskins made that day.

Of course there are always exceptions. Workington celebrated their three Wembley appearances in the 1950s by inviting the players involved to a reunion at the club at Easter, 1992. Three players and one wife ventured from Australia, including Bev Wilson from French Forest, New South Wales.

Bev was a second-row forward, like me, and therefore, though we played together in several matches, we were essentially competitors for a place in the side. On the whole, I think I probably had the edge on Bev. When I met him at the reunion I told him I was writing my autobiography and asked if he would write to me. His letter spoke of our days together. Bev was a typical second-rower, 6-foot-plus and weighing more than 14 stone, mobile, tenacious and tough. However, he is not at all a typical Australian; if he conforms to a type at all it is that of the English schoolmaster, traditional, conservative and re-served. He wrote this:

I remember one particular match we played together, and you scored a brace of tries against Liverpool. I gave you short passes from the ruck which sent you in full cry for the line, and seeing you disappear at high speed towards the try-line over some thirty to forty yards gave me a personal inner glow that only we sloggers in the tough stuff know.

That sort of generosity reflects real integrity. When players compete for a particular position there is usually a degree of selfishness, first to outshine your competitor, and second, to make sure he doesn't outshine you: you hardly want to contribute to his glory. Bev showed himself to be utterly selfless, first by allowing me the opportunity to excel, then by expressing his elation at my success.

One of the most flattering, and frightening, things that happened in my first eventful year with Workington was that I was asked to write a weekly article for a Rugby League paper. Each article was to consist of 1,000 words of finely wrought prose: I had barely written 1,000 words in my entire life up to then. Apprehensively, I accepted the challenge. There were problems to be overcome but, as I was slowly discovering, a problem can also be a challenge. The first challenge was my handwriting: unable to write cursively, I printed my 1,000 words. The second was that I had never until then been required to express myself in writing. It took me all my spare time in the following week to write my first article but to my astonishment, it was printed as I had written it, without change. This was a tremendous boost to my ego.

I covered the Rugby League news of Barrow, Whitehaven and Workington: I could not be everywhere at once so I gave a pound a week and extra to agents in Barrow and Whitehaven if they gave me good material. And I received a percentage of the sales as well as a fee for my articles. The next season I was asked to write for another Rugby League paper, again 1,000 words a week. By now, I had gained confidence in my journalism, while practice meant that my handwriting was becoming quite fluent.

My second article was written under a pseudonym and so two Manchester newspapers were paying me retainers for supplying exclusive news about the game. Of course I had to share what news I had equally between them to keep it exclusive! It then gradually occurred to me that I might soon be able to earn a living away from manual labour for the first time since leaving school.

Meanwhile, Gus's career at Workington was coming to an end. As he explains in his autobiography, he was keen to sign a new full-back, Bill Wookey, an eighteen-year-old who was playing for the Furness Rugby Union club, and whom, incidentally, I later signed for Barrow when I was manager there, after Wookey had been capped for Great Britain against Australia. That summer of 1954 Gus went with his family for a holiday to the south of France and in his absence discovered that the board had signed another full-back, Stan Thompson, from Dewsbury. As Gus writes, 'A manager's days are numbered when the directors sign players while he has an entirely different plan under consideration. No manager can stay in his job under conditions like that, so I offered my resignation – and it was accepted.'

Gus went briefly to Batley, then on to Salford as manager. For me, Gus Risman is the greatest player ever to have graced British Rugby League and stands majestic in the game's Hall of Fame in Rothwell, not far from Leeds. When Gus died on October 17, 1994 I was honoured to be asked to give the address at his funeral in Cockermouth. I told the congregation that exactly a month before I had visited Gus

at the residential home where he had lived after his wife's sudden death
and the stroke which had crippled him. On that last visit I had held
his hands – those hands which with a rugby ball had helped to bewitch
a multitude of opponents – and had looked into his eyes. He had
responded with a gentle smile, which was especially precious to me.
Over forty years before he had met me at Carlisle station for the first
time, to drive me to Workington. Little did either of us think then
what a profound effect those years would have on my future life. He
was the most self-disciplined man I have ever known, one of nature's
true gentlemen, and his spirit, I know, will always remain with me
and with all those who were privileged to know him.

Anyway, Gus was replaced as manager by Jim Brough, a dual Rugby
Union and Rugby League international, and at full-back by Stan
Thompson – the unwitting cause of all the trouble – who was a
window-cleaner by trade. As part of the transfer deal, Workington
bought Thompson a local window-cleaning round. He was rather a
taciturn chap but I had come a long way out of my shell by then and
we shared a surname. It made sense that we should combine his
window-cleaning skills with my local celebrity, but though I recognised
the prospects of a worthwhile partnership, I was reluctant to join him
at first, because I thought I was making a downward move socially.
Fortunately, I had enough sense to put that sort of snobbery aside, and
on our first day together we earned 17s. 6d. (75p) each, cleaning house
windows. But very quickly my status as a local hero brought in contracts
from around the county and soon we found that we had a real success
on our hands.

All in all, this was a dynamic and exciting time, a time of development and change. During my years at Workington one of the
friends I made was our prop forward, Andy Key. In 1989 Border TV
made a documentary film about my life, to which Andy contributed.
Border thought, correctly, that I would like to read what Andy had
written:

Cec and I became very good friends in the four years we played together at Workington Town, sharing our high points as well as our low ones. We roomed together on away trips and I saw at first hand how Cec began to educate himself. He would start by taking a *Reader's Digest* away with him on the team bus and would learn new words every trip. When the other lads were busy with cards or just generally chatting, I'd go and sit with him to test how well he'd learned the words and how to spell them.

I think he was a bit self-conscious, too, about his lack of education and his colour. To be quite honest it didn't matter to me if he was black; I know it may seem strange but I didn't really notice. He was accepted by the team as one of the boys, colour bars and racial problems were something we didn't have in west Cumbria.

But I do believe that the brashness, which Cec showed in company and which made him appear an extrovert, wasn't the real Cec. It was a bit of an act which he thought he had to put on to be accepted after his childhood and earlier life in Leeds. Underneath he was really a quiet man who could be easily hurt. On the field, for instance, I've seen him drop a ball and get a real roasting off one of the players. You could see him literally go into his shell. His confidence had been affected. I used to deliberately bring him back into the play as early as possible with a nicely-timed ball into the bread basket which he would take, and more often than not that would put him back on his game.

One of the main attributes he brought to the team was his competitiveness. In training, for instance, he didn't like to lose any of the sprints. He really put in a tremendous amount of effort and I don't think I would be exaggerating to say he put two or three yards on me as a result, for which I was extremely grateful.

Off the field, Cec was something of a practical joker and some of his pranks became legendary at the club. When we were playing in Lancashire we always used to stay in Southport and on the Friday night regularly used to go to the cinema. I can recall two occasions when he was thrown out by the commissionaire, al-

though I think it was probably because of the colour of his skin
rather than anything malicious in the prank.

On one occasion he had borrowed a bowler hat from the hotel
and was entertaining some of the film-goers with his own hilarious
version of the 'Amos and Andy Show' which was popular on TV
at the time. In those days there was an organ in the cinema which
occasionally sprang into life. Imagine our surprise on the night
Cec appeared at the organ, beaming with delight but apparently
not to the satisfaction of the commissionaire who promptly asked
him to leave.

I think the other occasion Andy may have been thinking of was when
I went to the toilet and saw a fully loaded ice-cream tray nearby. It
was almost time for the interval. I picked up the tray, adjusted the
strap around my neck, walked to the front of the cinema and popped
round the edge of the curtain. When the spotlight came on at my end
of the curtain, I appeared smack in the middle of the spotlight. I was
a star, my molars were all aglow; a big smile and a wave to my
colleagues brought a round of applause from them. I even managed
to sell two tubs of ice-cream before being unceremoniously hurled
out. What fun! Our manager, Jim Brough, was furious – which added
more mirth to the fun.

Another Workington team-mate, Ike Southward, one of the most
prolific try-scoring wingers of his day (his move from Workington to
Oldham involved a world-record transfer fee), also contributed to the
Border Television programme:

All the time I knew him, my old mate Cec was a fitness fanatic.
I would rate him as good a professional, because of his playing
and fitness attitude, as any who has donned the Town shirt. When
we were playing together there were few coloured players in
League, and that was a real problem which Cec had to overcome.
But he was a bit of a joker and, because of his bouncy smiling
character, he was always good for the morale of the team.

Cec's work rate and tackling were excellent and I rate him one of the fastest second-row forwards in the game at that time, equal to the great Geoff Gunney, Geoff Robinson or the illustrious Dick Huddart. In fact, he was so fast he often turned out for Town on the wing. On one occasion, I remember vividly, I was selected to play for the Army in a Rugby Union inter-services match at Twickenham during my national service and Cec was chosen in my place on the wing against Halifax. He had such an excellent game and received such reviews in the press that I began to wonder if I would get my place back. Luckily for me, Cec preferred to be with the forwards in the thick of all the action.

Sadly, not everything in my life was going so well. Being married to a dedicated sportsman can be a lonely life, as Barbara could testify. Professional Rugby League was and generally still is a semi-professional game; in other words, we had a job to do during the day. And alongside our full-time jobs there was training every Tuesday and Thursday evening, not to mention the home-wrecking away games. For most of these we would leave at 4.00 p.m. on Fridays, stay in a hotel on the Friday evening and not return until late on Saturday. Thus rugby occupied four nights a week for many weeks of the year.

Nor was I the perfect husband when I was around. I loathe domestic chores and have never been a practical person. My writing was another cause for disharmony: two articles a week left little time for domestic issues. The money I was earning from Rugby League both on and off the field did increase our standard of living dramatically, but there was a price to pay. We never seemed to suffer the tensions you might expect of a mixed marriage. Instead, we were separated by something far more conventional, far more universal: we just stopped caring enough for one another. Our marriage was already over before we decided, amicably, and with relief, that we should go our separate ways.

The divorce went through smoothly but it was a sad time nonetheless. Our home was vacated, our furniture sold. We had invested a lot of faith in our future together and somehow that faith had been wasted. I lodged with a friend, Walker Jackson, his wife Maureen, and their baby. They lived in a small terrace house with no room even for a toilet inside, never mind for a lumbering 6-foot rugby player. But Cumbrians are wonderfully warm-hearted people and the Jacksons picked me up and sorted me out.

However, there is usually a positive to follow a negative, and here there were two. For I not only learned that there were wonderful people like the Jacksons in the world but I also discovered that I had an instinctive interest in the arts. For now Barbara had gone there was an emptiness in my life, and I tried to fill this by concentrating more on things like music and literature. It was strange how much spare time I had now. Barbara had accused me of giving no time to our marriage; yet apparently I had given it plenty because I was suddenly able to join the local music society, operatic society and arts club. I was enthusiastic, I was enjoying myself, and above all I was appreciated. It was beginning to dawn on me that maybe I wasn't just a stupid black oaf and that what I missed was not so much brains as education. Gradually, unstoppably, my obsession with education was beginning.

1. My Rugby League career is well under way, 1949. Les Williams, a PE teacher who used to supervise Hunslet training, discovers that I am the fastest sprinter on the club's books. *(Left to right):* Tommy Potter, Brian Shaw, myself, Ted Carroll (of the famous nose), Alan Snowden

2. Hunslet *v.* Bramley, 1951. I'm on the ground, having helped Bill Metcalfe to bring down a Bramley player. Following up are Eddie Bennett and Ted Carroll

3. The Hunslet first team, 1951. *(Back row, left to right):* Don Rees, Granville James, myself, Eddie Bennett, Walter Burnell, Gordon Waite, Jack Evans; *(front row)* Les Williams, Tosh Thornton, Alf Burnell, Arthur Talbot, Freddie Williamson

4. The Great Britain team is presented to the New Zealand High Commissioner by the team captain Jack Cunliffe (Wigan) before the first Test at Odsal, 1951. *(Right to left):* Ken Gee (Wigan), myself, Alf Burnell (Hunslet) shaking the High Commissioner's hand, and Dickie Williams (Leeds)

5. Helped by hooker Vince McKeating (Workington Town), I bring down a New Zealand player in the first Test at Odsal, won by Great Britain 21–15

6. Ken Gee (Wigan) shakes hands with the New Zealand captain, McKenzie, after the first Test at Odsal, as the teams troop off. I suffered slight concussion in the match and Alf Burnell, my Hunslet team-mate, holds on to my jersey

7. Alf Burnell (Hunslet), Ken Traill (Bradford Northern), myself, and Dickie Williams (Leeds) at Leeds station leaving for Swinton and the second Test against New Zealand, 1951. Great Britain won again, this time by 20–19

8. Workington Town *v.* Warrington, 1953, on a dreadful day in my first season with Town. I am running hard at the Warrington defence, while, in the centre of the picture, Town's Brian Edgar (no. 11) effectively obstructs Harry Bath's attempts to tackle me

9. Gus Risman, my ideal of a professional sportsman, holds high the Challenge Cup after Workington Town had beaten Featherstone Rovers 18–10 at Wembley after the 1952 final. Tony Paskins, the Australian centre, is on the left

10. Workington Town v. Hull, 1956. I outpace Hull's Johnny Whiteley to score a good try

11. Workington Town *v.* Oldham, 1957. The players, *left to right,* are Doug Holland, Syd Little (Oldham), Brian Edgar (with the ball), Norman Herbert, myself, Jack Keith (the Oldham hooker on the ground) and Bill Lymer

12. Workington Town *v.* Halifax, 1957. The Town players, *left to right,* are Sol Roper, Andy Key, myself, Brian Edgar and Eppie Gibson, who is about to congratulate me on scoring the only try that afternoon

13. Sol Roper introduces the Workington Town team to the American Ambassador before the start of 1958 Challenge Cup final at Wembley. Andy Key is shaking hands in the photograph and on his right are Brian Edgar, then myself. In the background is the Town chairman, Jim Graves

14. Wigan break through the Town defence in the 1958 Challenge Cup final. The Town players, *from left to right,* are Ike Southward, John (Loppy Lugs) O'Neill, Sol Roper and myself

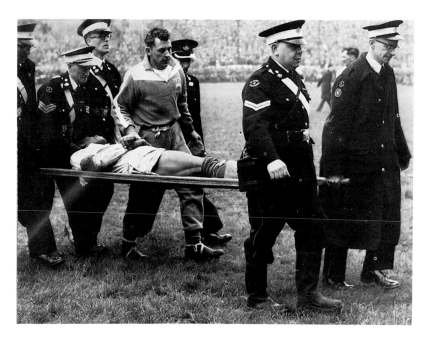

15. I am carried off at Odsal in the Championship final, 1958. It was the end of my playing career

16. Though my serious injury at the 1958 Championship final prevented me from playing competitive Rugby League again, I was only too pleased to devote as much time as I could to coaching the game in youth clubs

Chapter 4

Back on the rugby field, though Gus had retired we were still a good team, a great team even. With Gus to lift us we had played like men possessed; but without him, though our results were good, playing sometimes became a bit of a burden. I always hated the weather from December to February. The pitches are muddy enough in October and November but at least it is warm, though the ground does get churned up. Unfortunately the furrows freeze in December and seem not to thaw until February. It must be the half-share of Caribbean blood within me which makes me detest the cold so much. I used to shudder in bed when I heard, the morning before a match, the fierce, howling winds that announced the ice.

Handling the ball in such conditions was terrifying, but not getting involved in the game was even worse. Scrummaging, placing one's head between two pairs of mud-sodden shorts, was beyond all reason. These were beastly conditions: perishing cold fingers, all feeling frozen out; icy, wet, muddy shorts clinging to thighs; hair matted with freezing, slushy mud; body shaking and trembling uncontrollably; trying to clear the mud from hands by wiping them on the jersey and succeeding only in muddying the jersey even more. Only the whites of my eyes seemed free of mud.

My worst nightmare was playing for Workington on Boxing Day in 1956 at Barrow on ground that was awash with thick mud from melting snow. It was churned up into a gigantic mud pond. Our forwards were bogged down, defending our try-line (this was long before the six-tackle rule was introduced). Darkie Thompson did not exist; there were just twelve mud-sodden forwards. I was having a sort of fit from exposure to these horrendous conditions, having to take my turn in taking the ball, making sure we kept possession, thus making

sure the opposition could not score a snap try. I gathered the ball, six
Barrow forwards shaped up to pound into my defenceless body, smack-
ing me down into the mud. Twelve forwards stayed in a small patch
of mud; this was sheer stupidity, madness even. For forty minutes, each
half, there was nowhere to win relief from this lunacy, this suffering.
The strange thing was that the other forwards seemed to be revelling
in the mud. Since everyone was dragged down to the same level, the
talented players could not shine and the more pedestrian were in their
glory.

Mud squelched in our boots, and filled our eyes and ears; I became
a shambles of a human being, a pathetic sight. We performed like the
inmates of a mental asylum, mindless motions in a sea of mud. I tried
gripping my fingers to the palms of my hands and opening them again
to try to get some circulation going. I felt as though my blood had
frozen, each finger felt like a separate icicle. Oh Lord, have mercy on
me! It was sheer misery. I was freezing throughout my body. It is
amazing I recovered sufficiently to be able to tell this story. I did not
care who won; just *please* blow the final whistle. I felt bovine-like,
wandering aimlessly. What foolishness, standing helpless, unable to take
a stride forward before being hammered into the mud and, my God,
did it hurt. There was no protection from the six huge forwards still
crashing like battering rams into my weak and shivering body. This
continuous battering was excruciating, with a cold, icy wind howling
round my flailing torso. I could not withstand these conditions much
longer; I would die of exposure. God, why am I doing this? If I had
died at that very moment, it would have been a relief. I had no desire
to live and I longed for an instantaneous escape from this man-torture.
Each hand was now so frozen that I was simply a useless lump of meat.

The referee was human after all. He blew up before the official
time. I am sure my life was saved by that decision. But now the worst
was to come. I had become dehumanised, had lost all feeling. I usually
have burning aches if I go into hot water too soon. But on this occasion,
once the pain had reached my extremities, it was a living hell. I let
out a silent scream. I shed tears freely like a baby, holding my head

low so that no one could see the condition I was in. I was again a
loner. No words can describe my pain and mental agony. My bootlaces
were cut open to remove my boots and my fingers and toes were
massaged with towels. I was the only one who suffered; was it my
Afro-Caribbean blood that caused me such agony?

But perhaps I wouldn't have worried too much about those appalling
conditions had I known what triumphs lay ahead. In many ways the
1957–58 season was Workington's vintage year; it was certainly a season
which shines out over my whole career like the North Star on a clear
night. I didn't miss a match that year, which was packed with hopes,
fears and disappointments. I scored thirteen tries, set up a club record
for a forward by scoring four tries against Blackpool and a hat-trick
against one of the stronger teams, Widnes. For my third try in that
match, my friend Andy Key, the prop forward who was so difficult
to tackle, suddenly burst through the opposition and was accelerating
to the try-line with only fifteen yards to go. I was haring up in close
support when he had only the full-back to beat. I yelled, 'Andy, let's
have the ball.' It was an easy try for me, and a hat-trick too. After the
match, I thought of that time when my second-row partner at Hunslet
had selfishly hung on to the ball when I was in the clear for an
unopposed try and he was tackled short of the line.

There had been no less than ten internationals in the team when
Gus Risman was playing but great though that team was, the 1957–58
side, made up mainly of Cumbrians, with only two internationals –
Ike Southward and myself – broke records which the previous side
had never touched. That great side consisted of a group of men drawn
together first by an unyielding desire for success and then by friendship.
It was sheer joy to be in their company.

We achieved two particularly remarkable feats. First, we went for
no less than twenty-three games without defeat (which still stands as
a club record); and we reached the two principal cup finals: the
Challenge Cup final against Wigan at Wembley and the League Championship final against Hull at Odsal. In addition, four Workington
players – Harry Archer, Brian Edgar, Ike Southward and Bill Wookey –

were included in the 1958 Great Britain touring party to Australia; I missed selection to go with my second-row partner, Brian Edgar, by one vote in the Selection Committee debate. Moreover, the club coach, Jim Brough, was included as the British team coach and our chairman, Tom Mitchell, who was that year president of the Rugby Football League, also accompanied the party as manager.

Looking back, and ignoring my own contribution, I can only agree that that was a very special Workington side. Perhaps two players in particular stand out: Sol Roper, our diminutive scrum-half who rarely missed a tackle, and who later became the youngest captain to play at Wembley, and Brian Edgar, who was later given the Freedom of Workington and went on three Australasian tours.

Brian was the last of four brilliant second-row forwards whom I was fortunate enough to have partnered. At Hunslet, there was Ted Carroll (of whom more later) and Geoff Gunney MBE, a player with all the skills and speed any coach could ask for; and at Workington, my first partner had been my Australian friend John Mudge, a tenacious tackler, a reliable handler of the ball, and extremely fast both in movement and wit, and then finally Brian, a product of Cockermouth Grammar School. Cumbria has produced many fine forwards and Brian was from the top drawer. I owe much to these men: it was inspirational to play alongside them. They made many tries for me and at the same time they were invariably in support if I made a break.

The semi-final of the Challenge Cup that year was against Feather-stone Rovers at the Odsal stadium in Bradford. But the prestige and importance of a semi-final made no difference to the weather conditions. A rainstorm had made the pitch the familiar quagmire and, to top that, the night before the match, I contracted 'flu in our Ilkley hotel. But having reached this far in the competition, we went to enormous lengths to field the strongest possible side. Minor injuries got strapped; the walking wounded were given pain-killers. I was drugged before going out to play but the pain-killer did not dull my senses too much and we had a great game that ended with a famous 8–2 victory. And so we were on our way to Wembley.

Not only that, but we were also among the top four clubs who were to play off for the League Championship. As there were thirty-two teams in the League in those days, to have got that far was in itself a real achievement. And we had already met and beaten a star-studded Leeds team in the first round of the Challenge Cup at Headingley. The Leeds centre that day was the incomparable Lewis Jones. Jones was a genius, a fabulous entertainer and a fantastic match winner. He had blistering speed off the mark, a keen eye for an opening, a phenomenal sense of anticipation, magical hands, nimble footwork and an amazing kick. His most remarkable feat was the ability to change gear in mid air with a sudden flick of his legs which baffled many a defence. Lewis Jones had the art of making the impossible possible. All we had opposite him was a pasty-faced, lanky, local lad called John O'Neill by his parents and teachers, though we had rechristened him Loppy Lugs after the successful racehorse of that period. It was no contest. Loppy Lugs thrashed Lewis Jones.

On the Saturday before our Wembley final we played St Helens on their ground in the semi-final of the Championship play-offs. The Saints were a star-studded team which included Alex Murphy, Alan Prescott and Vince Karalius. I told my teammates to relax if either team got too far ahead and so avoid possible serious injury before Wembley. But things refused to work out that way. We were only one point behind at half-time, and the lead kept changing with a series of drop-goals in the second half, worth 2 points in those days. With three minutes to go, we were one point behind. The Saints, believing attack to be the best form of defence, had camped thirteen men on our 25-yard line when Norman Herbert, our prop forward, broke through their cordon. St Helens were completely thrown by this surprise development and Herbert scored beneath their posts, giving us the match. We were now in the final of the Championship, timed to take place one week after the Wembley final.

After the St Helens game the Saints' skipper, Alex Murphy, had tears of frustration and disappointment in his eyes. Of course Alex later went on to become a latter-day Eddie Waring, sharing his vast experience and analytical knowledge of the modern game with a national television audience. 'Remember that game, Alex?' I remind him when we meet. He replies, 'I wish you'd shut your bluddy gob about that bluddy game. But I was a good'un for a little chap, weren't I?' He certainly was.

One thing we had learned in that remarkable season was to take one game at a time, but even so I don't believe there was a single one of us, who, in that week before Wembley, did not dream or daydream of scoring a winning try or of making a last-ditch saving tackle. The Championship final was not in our thoughts: we could forget about that for a while. Only Wembley beckoned. Our lives changed. We all took days off work for extra training on the shores of the Solway Firth. There was tea in the clubhouse before we were sent off by the fans to our expensive hotel on the London periphery. Suddenly we were in the dressing-room at Wembley. The coach tried to play down the stress and tension. It didn't matter what he said. Everyone was busy with private thoughts. We lined up in the tunnel, paused, then went out into the arena. It was difficult to control our emotion as our names were called out to the roar of the crowd. We were proud, and rightly so. Considering we were such a young team, and considering too that we no longer had Gus Risman's inspiration to guide us, it was a truly magnificent achievement on our part to have got there. For the record, the Workington team that day was: McAvoy; Wookey, Leatherbarrow, O'Neill, Southward; Archer, Roper; Herbert, Eden, Key, Thompson, Edgar and Eve.

We lined up for the start. All nerves were stretched taut. We were desperate to get on with the game. The noise was deafening. Then play began. Somehow we started to move the ball around, mechanically at first, but almost immediately Ike Southward set the stadium on fire with a splendid runaway try after Edgar had paved the way. Edgar side-stepped two men, and passed the ball to Southward on the halfway-line. Ike then came inside Wigan's Mick Sullivan, beat him hands down for speed and crashed over for a wonderful try, which he converted himself. What a start: within ten minutes Workington were leading

5–0. Ike later kicked two goals and so was responsible for all of Workington's 9 points.

Then, as a post-match report put it, 'The cruellest blow hit Town: injury free for so long, they lost their off-half tactician, Harry Archer'. He was carried off with severe concussion after a stiff-arm tackle by Mick Sullivan. What a start – but what a handicap for the rest of the game as no replacements were allowed in those days. Southward tried for an interception which failed and allowed Sullivan to score. Then Edgar was seen to be lying prone after a scrummage; he picked himself up only to totter dazedly around and had to be helped from the field. But trainer Whalley had hardly got Edgar to the touchline when he was called back to give attention to Key who was also seen to be lying senseless. This now gave Wigan a huge numerical advantage.

Edgar came back after eighteen minutes and there was a howl from the crowd as fists flew, but within seconds Wigan had scored again. McTigue went over after Herbert had missed a tackle. Key came back on but then had to go to the trainer's dugout again to receive more attention. It had been many months since a team had put three tries through the Workington defence and Wigan were monopolising the scrums. I broke away and passed to McAvoy steaming up in support on Wookey's wing, but the winger was nowhere in support. Then we nearly grabbed back the lead. Southward had virtually grounded the ball – which would have meant a try to us, and a conversion would have given us the Cup – when Norman Cherrington, the Wigan second-row forward, with a brilliant piece of cover work, tapped Southward's ankles. Ike dropped the ball as he was about to ground it and we lost 9–13.

Many of the boys shed tears in the dressing-room. It was not easy to watch our opponents collecting the Cup and their winners' medals, then running a lap of honour, surrounded by a sea of photographers. After such a successful season, defeat at this stage was a body blow. We applauded the victors but in the dressing-room there was deathly silence, the players sitting too exhausted and downhearted to take off their playing kit. Mr Graves, the club chairman, spoke quietly, 'Don't let it get you down, boys; you have not disgraced yourselves; indeed you have made me proud. We will make amends next Saturday. Let's have a good time tonight and get it out of your system and prepare yourselves for celebration seven days from now.' So we had lost, but the fans back at Workington did us proud, and Workington Borough Council gave us a civic reception, just as if we had won the Cup.

Then the following Saturday we faced Hull in the Championship final. It was a great achievement to have reached Wembley but an even greater one to have got to Odsal, depending as the Championship final does on good results throughout the season, on the lush grounds of August through to October, and on the cold, muddy and frost-bound grounds of winter. This puts a tremendous strain on any side. The extra games which have to be played build up towards the end of the season so there is extra training as well as mid-week matches every week. I played in every game that season and I was also keeping a window-cleaning business going and was also rock climbing. We had played forty-seven matches in all from August to May and now all that was left was the Championship final.

However, my season ended, certainly my Championship final ended, when I went down with seriously damaged ligaments in my knee in the twenty-fifth minute of the match. As the *Sunday Express* reported:

Until Cec Thompson was carried off in the twenty-fifth minute, I felt confident that Workington were set for the title. Thompson had been the dynamo driving their pack and without him, twelve exhausted, flat-footed players trailed off the field yesterday, clutching their second set of losers' medals within eight days. There was really no hope for them after Thompson's injury. Workington's coloured second-row forward went into a tackle on Hull's Cyril Sykes, catapulted over him and rolled on his back in agony, clutching his left leg. He went off on a stretcher to the roars of applause which his driving forward skills so richly deserve. In hospital, torn ligaments were diagnosed.

Yet Workington had stormed into the lead before poor

Thompson had been put into the ambulance. Mighty, magnificent Brian Edgar slipped miraculously past a couple of defenders to send Ike Southward racing thirty-five yards for the Hull line. But it was only a despairing gesture of defiance. Whatever Workington tried went wrong. That jinx that rode on their backs at Wembley last week was still with them yesterday and they lost 3–20.

The *Sunday Despatch* reported:

'Workington never had a chance without Cec. His injury happened in the twenty-fifth minute when the score sheet was blank and Workington had shown a lot of good play. Hull had hardly been in Workington's half up to that point. Workington then had to face a fit, fast and powerful thirteen-man team with only twelve players. It was a hopeless task though they fought gallantly and did not yield until Johnny Whiteley, the Hull loose forward, went through under the posts without a hand being laid on him.

Yorkshire Sports had this to say:

Hull had won the title in 1956 by one point and lost by a similar margin last season, starting slight favourites on this occasion. Workington suffered a severe blow when Thompson went down in a heavy tackle and hit the ground hard. He lay writhing on the pitch, holding his left leg, and had to be carried off on a stretcher. This came after twenty-five minutes of keen duelling in which neither side had looked like scoring. Until Thompson's accident Town's pack had been more than a match for Hull's powerhouse six. But without their most skilled tactician and ball distributor, Workington had to set defiance to adversity but failed.

Over the last four consecutive Saturdays much energy had been sapped from Workington's players. They were a young, new team, most of them Cumbrian-born. In the Championship play-offs, they had met Oldham away, followed by St Helens away in the semi-final; then they had to play Wigan at Wembley and, finally, Hull in the Championship final. Many clubs with stronger reserve strength would have shuddered at such a titanic programme. But these local youngsters had been moulded into a sturdy fighting force and had fought their way to two of the highest honours of the game – beaten in both finals but not disgraced. It had been a great achievement.

The teams in the Championship final that day were:

Workington Town: McAvoy; Southward, O'Neill, Leatherbarrow, Faulder; Archer, Roper; Herbert, Eden, Stamper, Edgar, Thompson, Eve

Hull: Bateson; Watts, Cooper, Saville, Dannat; Broadhurst, Finn; Scott, Holdstock, Hambling, P. Whiteley, Sykes, J. Whiteley

My knee was pretty badly damaged. After twelve years of first-class rugby I was at a loss. Apart from the fractured leg in my first season I had enjoyed an almost injury-free career. Was I now to earn my living purely from my window-cleaning business? I didn't relish the prospect. Climbing ladders would hardly help my injured knee. Local stardom would soon evaporate. For some time I had wondered how I was to get away from the harsh world of rugby; now I had the opportunity, and did not want to take it. There was more than money, popularity or comradeship involved in my reluctance. Rugby League had become part of the fabric of my life and had given me some status in society. Was I now to be a nobody again?

However, there was no point in trying to fight the inevitable. Having few natural skills I had relied on fitness and guile to retain my place in the team, and now the fitness was gone. I played only thirty-two games all told during the next two seasons, 1958-60, and made a hopeless attempt to start the following season with just a single game against Bradford Northern. Then my retirement was announced in the local press. But in the afternoon of the very same day a telegram arrived inviting me to take over the coaching of Barrow. I wasn't really interested so I told the club that their terms were insufficient and that I wanted twice the salary they had offered. I waited for their refusal; instead there was another telegram for me with the one word: 'Accepted'.

I had had some preparation for coaching. I had been to an RFL summer coaching course at Lilleshall under the eye of the RFL secretary at that time, Bill Fallowfield – with such stars as Colin Hutton of Hull, Laurie Gant, formerly a team-mate of mine at Hunslet but then with Featherstone, and Peter Ramsden of Huddersfield as fellow pupils – and had won a first-class diploma in readiness for the end of my playing days. And I had already taken an eighteen-month physiotherapy course, gaining a certificate of proficiency after a week of practical examinations at a college in Maidenhead.

It was during the Lilleshall coaching course that I met someone who became and has remained my closest friend. Wilbur Athersmith was the secretary of Ulverston Hospital and lived in that delightful unspoilt town in the south-west of the Lake District. He was also a Rugby League stalwart, giving the bulk of his spare time to the amateur game in that part of the north-west. Because of this he invited me to come to his club, where I gave a talk, did some coaching, and presented the trophies at the club's annual dinner. After that we went together to Lilleshall on that coaching course.

The days were exhausting, the nights were hectic, and by the end of that week we needed a holiday. So we took it in turns to sleep or drive going back home to Barrow in my two-seater sports MG, and the friendship that began during that long drive has developed to the point where Wilbur has become my alter ego and my second conscience. He is the one whose advice I need when I am at a psychological low – a man of intense integrity who is unflappable, wise, conventional, yet flexible in his sympathies. Our natures are completely different, which perhaps is why our friendship has always remained so close.

Anyway, I soon realised that what I knew about the game of Rugby League was less important than what I knew about people. There is always an element of public relations involved in running a team: cups have to be presented to the local amateur teams, there is coaching to be carried out in other parts of the county and the media has to be fed and kept satisfied. Less conventional exercises in public relations are also needed sometimes in a close-knit community such as Barrow-in-Furness. If you drop a player, the whole clan can go gunning for you. Likewise the coach has to be a psychologist, drawing on his own experience as a player to understand what is going on in the team: there are old players who will be using their wits to disguise their weaknesses, and young players whose enthusiasm is likely to cripple them if they don't slow down. What I learned about man management and psychology at Barrow has stood me in good stead ever since.

My appointment at Barrow meant moving to that town but my contract allowed me to have Wednesdays free each week to attend to my cleaning business. I now had a labour force of four. Back in 1957 Stan Thompson had struck a run of bad form and began to feel unsettled in Workington. He wanted to go back to his native West Yorkshire, and I was happy to use my sports column to help him. I was even happier to buy him out of our business. However, I still needed help, so I asked a chap whom we shall call Jim if he would like to work for me.

'It would be a privilege to work for you, Cec, and wonderful to get out of the muck of the mill.' He had no qualifications from his schooling; he was just an unskilled labourer. But he was a bright lad and a hard worker, so I offered him a substantial increase in his pay, with prospects of it doubling, trebling, or increasing even more as the business expanded.

Later, Jim's brother joined the staff as did my old Workington team-mate, Harry Archer, on his return from the Australasian tour with Great Britain; and I also had a man, Joe Newton, chimney-sweeping.

I asked Jim if he would be the business manager. 'Thanks for having faith in me,' he said. 'You've always been good to me.' It was true. I remember his wife Betty in tears because, though I paid a good wage, they were under real financial pressure; I lent them £100 to repay at their leisure. 'You will always be able to rely on me,' he added.

I still took an active part in the business when I could. Even today it is a source of pride for me that though I am now managing director, along the way I have been involved in every aspect of the business. I even became – so far as I know – the only genuine black chimney-sweep in the country. I read an advertisement that boasted, 'Raise your earning power with this chimney-sweeping equipment,' and, thinking this would be useful, I duly travelled to London and purchased the stuff. That was when I took on Joe Newton. Cleaning chimneys of new properties was easy since the flues are vertical. However, older buildings have crooked chimneys in them, and sometimes the brushes got stuck. Then Joe would telephone me for help: I really dreaded those calls, especially in winter time.

On one occasion Joe needed help on an old two-storey building. It was, inevitably, an icy cold February morning after a night of heavy snow. Joe went up a standard ladder to get to the roof and took a cat ladder with him. I watched as he fixed the cat ladder to the ridge of the roof and climbed it to the chimney; then I followed up and on to the lower part of the cat ladder, intending to help Joe free the brushes. Our breath vaporised as soon as it left our mouths, confirming the intensity of the cold. But the cat ladder was not as firmly fixed as we had thought: in fact it was fastened to a pocket of snow. My weight was too much for it; it suddenly slipped off the point of the roof and swung sideways, diagonally across the roof.

'What the hell are you doing?' Joe yelled. 'You'll have us both killed.' He was shaking violently.

'Keep still,' I yelled back. 'You're making the ladder slip further.'

'I can't,' he insisted. I tried to calm him down. At the same time I thought, 'If this ladder falls any further, I'll jump.' Better to have two broken legs than fall head first. There would be no choice for

Joe: he was a short dumpling of a bloke, and still trembling violently. I yelled, 'For goodness sake, relax.' A large crowd had now gathered on the street below: it was vastly entertaining for them and rather like being at the speedway, which is always most exciting when the riders fall off. They led pretty uneventful lives, those housewives, and now here was a chance to watch a couple of chaps break their necks.

Back at the drama Joe whispered, 'I think I've shit myself.'

'That's good,' I told him. 'Now maybe you'll relax.'

At last the fire brigade arrived. The firemen insisted that I be rescued first, though I put up some resistance. In chorus they cried, 'Your colleague didn't play for Workington!'

Being a local hero still had its advantages, though by then I was not spending much time in Workington. Once a week I stayed with Jim, having a couple of beers and discussing business, but the rest of the time I was coaching Barrow.

There were about forty players on the staff at Barrow. There were also fifteen committee members, and most of them needed to be managed more than the players. A few youngish, more progressive directors gave some hope for change but they were outnumbered by the dinosaur brigade. The seventy-year-old chairman, with his leathery, wrinkled face, was a sort of brontosaurus. Whenever he became anxious, which was often, he would grind his upper and lower dental plates so that they slipped regularly from his mouth. He had little enthusiasm for forward planning; indeed, he positively impeded progress. Even more useless was the club secretary.

Barrow had enjoyed a proud history with a record of brilliant players, especially my predecessor, Willie Horne, probably the most outstanding player ever to have graced the Barrow club. He had played twenty-four times for Great Britain and made 462 appearances for Barrow, scoring 112 tries and kicking 741 goals. He was a gentleman on and off the field but he lacked the charisma needed for coaching, especially after the club had declined from being the highly successful Challenge Cup winners against Workington in 1955 to become a pretty nondescript outfit during the next four years. Willie retired in 1959.

Team selection took place on Thursdays. But it was not long before I realised that most of the decisions were made on the telephone much earlier in the week. I always needed eight votes if I was to have my way. So who was a freemason? A leftie? A right-winger? A trade-unionist? A drinker? A ditherer? By doing my homework beforehand, the meetings themselves became much more malleable.

Not surprisingly, it was the conservative group of directors who bore most heavily upon me and I needed all my animal cunning during the confrontations that soon started. So far as I can remember, there was no window in the boardroom and when all the directors met at their weekly assembly, the room was dark with cigar, pipe and cigarette smoke, mingled with the stench of snuff in hot weather and with the added attraction of the smell from sweating bodies. My independent income from the cleaning company probably allowed me to be rather more forthright in discussion than if I had depended, in this literally stifling atmosphere, only on my club salary. But it was an uphill struggle.

The chairman had little experience of finance or business affairs, beyond his modest, prudent, conventional and comfortable teaching career. He resented me having a brand new MG sports car, a beautiful young girl-friend (of whom much more later), freshly back from a month's holiday on the continent, a holiday which had included the Rome Olympics and the Oberammagau passion play. However, I think I helped to improve committee-player harmony a bit. Occasionally, to avoid the sportscoat-and-flannels-with-mac-over-the-arm approach, and judging it to be a good deal more professional, I would insist that I met a potential new signing by dining in a smart hotel with my girl-friend and with the player and his partner.

Some twenty years later, I visited Barrow as a director of the newly formed Mansfield Marksman RLFC and, lo and behold, things had hardly changed. There was a magnificent playing area, but going to the boardroom was like visiting Death Row: women were excluded and that old familiar stench prevailed. The club safe was still the back trouser pocket of the same elderly official, short and squat and greying.

The wad of notes was so huge that he waddled along as though *rigor mortis* had set in his buttocks many years before.

On the playing side, when I took over, there was an outstanding winger who became an international and a tourist, following in the same footsteps as his father, except that his father, Bill Burgess senior, had been a forward. Bill Burgess junior was a law unto himself, with his own magical talents, something which could not be coached. He won fourteen caps for Great Britain and played absolutely instinctively, so I simply had to turn a blind eye to some of his antics. His phenomenal speed and abundance of nervous energy gave him an explosive force off the mark and he was gifted with a natural change of pace.

However, I could not allow this young player, blessed with above average intelligence, to think that he could have everything his own way. I had just a toehold of authority over him and that toehold could easily slip away if I made a wrong move in our delicate relationship. I had great respect for Bill but I was careful to see that that respect was reciprocated. In fact, Bill and I spoke little during training sessions. I think this was partly because he and I recognised that most of what people say to each other in life is a load of rubbish anyway but partly also because each signalled telepathically to the other, 'It's better to compromise than confront.' He went his way and I mine. I found facing up to that kind of coach-player problem extremely interesting; indeed, all my new managerial responsibilities – the need for tact in dealing with the older, more senior, players, especially in front of the youngsters, and a need to listen to everyone's personal problems on and off the field – were exceptionally stimulating.

As it happens, I spoke to Billy Burgess again only the other day on the telephone, after a gap of almost thirty years. We recalled the fearful occasion on which he had almost died on the field. Billy had collided head on with a Huddersfield player in a mid-week match at Fartown. He lay writhing on the ground, his eyeballs had disappeared, and saliva was pouring from his mouth. He had partially swallowed his tongue, was having great difficulty in breathing and was gradually choking to death. Fortunately the arrival of a doctor saved the situation. Bill's breathing gradually returned to normal and an ambulance took him to hospital where he remained overnight.

It was during this same telephone conversation that Bill told me an interesting story about skin pigmentation. During our time together at Barrow, the club signed a jet-black South African, Duncan Pikoli. He played on the opposite wing to Burgess, and after I had left the club Duncan told Billy that he had found it difficult to take orders from me since he was a true African, while I was of mixed blood, a 'coloured', and thus in tribal terms inferior to him. So I learned that apparently I am perpetually inferior, whether in white society or black!

Burgess later signed for Salford and his superiority blossomed when he escaped from those terrible twins, the Barrow chairman and secretary, to grow to full stature under Brian Snape. That same superiority was fulfilled outside the game too since Billy is now senior lecturer at Furness College, the proud possessor of three degrees and three sons, one at university in the USA and one about to follow. This sort of growth through the opportunities provided by Rugby League makes me very happy. I only wish there was more of this upward social mobility, this realisation of true potential.

I was still supplying weekly Rugby League news to the Manchester press, covering Barrow, Workington and Whitehaven, when I suddenly became aware that there was a mole leaking material from Barrow boardroom discussions to Manchester. I strongly suspected the club secretary. An ideal opportunity arose to snuff out this leakage when he and I travelled to London to sign Pikoli when he arrived from South Africa. When I challenged the secretary, eyeball to eyeball, he flatly denied the allegation, yet from that day onwards the leakage stopped.

As time went on I became increasingly frustrated. My parsimonious chairman delayed signing new players and the standards of our otherwise pretty mediocre team dropped still further. After a decade of success, it was hard to swallow mediocrity on the field. Indeed, there were times when my continuing contract was difficult to endure. Occasionally there was some blue sky between the dark clouds but it did not last long enough to give me much hope. The players were fantastic, eager to improve their game, respectful and polite, individually and collectively, but I was in the doldrums. I knew I had to get away from Barrow. I was blaming myself whenever the team lost, and an unpleasant weekend always followed.

I played twice for Barrow in the two seasons I was there, against Bramley and Blackpool. On both occasions, I simply filled in when we were desperately short of players through injury; and the Blackpool game proved to be not only a melancholy occasion but my last in Rugby League. In those days Blackpool were always regarded as an easy win for the opposition, and in the 1957–58 season I had scored no less than four tries against them for Workington, a feat which was not only a personal best but a Workington club record for a forward. In 1962, however, Barrow lost the match at the seaside town and it was entirely my fault. Barrow were leading by 2 points with seconds to go but Blackpool were encamped on our line and we were under severe pressure.

I had the reputation throughout the game of stealing possession at the play-the-ball by racing round the player playing the ball and smothering the player who was supposed to receive it. I had done this successfully on numerous occasions and saw no reason why I should not succeed again, even against the Blackpool captain, Tommy Bishop, soon to become an outstanding scrum-half for Great Britain and St Helens. Unfortunately the wily Bishop out-thought me by tapping the ball forward and touching down for a try in the split second in which I had leapt forward in the hope of tackling the receiver and taking the ball from him. It was an humiliating defeat by that season's wooden-spooners; the atmosphere on the team bus going home was dreadful and the *Barrow Mail*'s reporter was unforgiving.

I had had enough of Barrow after that match. But what was I to do? Clearly, for a start, I had to educate myself. So I picked the brains of one of the players who was a teacher and he explained to me the intricacy of the levels 'O' and 'A' and confirmed that one could not get very far in any direction without English 'O' level. So it was that

I enrolled at Workington Technical College, joining a nurses' course to get English 'O' level in one year, and at the same time began a correspondence course. A routine began. Each morning I would work at my correspondence course from 6 a.m. to 8 a.m. Every Wednesday I drove up the coast road from Barrow to Workington, and not just to see Jim: I did not want anyone to know what I was doing in case I was ridiculed. That might have undermined my secret ambition to become a full-time student and then, one day perhaps, a PE teacher. One essay I had to write was about an historic building of my choice. I chose Furness Abbey and used the local library for my research. I learned a lot of things I should probably have learned much earlier. I did not even know that the country was divided into local authorities, and yet our chairman was then the mayor of Barrow.

I continued for a year like that, and then came the examination, and the result: grade A for 'O' level English. I could do it! I could pass exams! Now I was determined to waste no more time with the life I had been leading and I searched for a college I could attend. Huddersfield Technical College (now Huddersfield University) ran a four-year course, consisting of seven 'O' levels and three 'A' levels for fourteen-year-olds who had failed the Eleven Plus and who belonged to the West Riding of Yorkshire. I fulfilled only half the conditions but I applied nonetheless and was offered an interview.

Twelve years of confidence, hard won on the rugby field, melted as I paused outside the college before that interview. At school I had been overawed and afraid of the teachers, and the headmaster had seemed such a very elevated person, so far above me that he was virtually a different species. Now I was that schoolboy all over again as I walked up and down outside the building. At last I overcame my fear, swallowing the saliva in my mouth, squeezing my clenched fists, and telling myself to 'Relax, relax'. My fingernails were almost cutting into my flesh and I was sweating profusely as I normally do on such occasions. They asked for my qualifications: 'O' level English grade A, a first-class Rugby League coaching certificate, a physiotherapy certificate, and my St John's Ambulance first-aid certificate: I really had no way of knowing how perfectly ridiculous that list must have seemed to them. But all was not lost. The director of studies for the course, Mr Mollan, was keen on sport and had played cricket with someone who had played for Hunslet in a minor way. I was accepted on condition that I could pass the entrance examination for the following subjects: English, history, geography, biology and mathematics. Mollan looked at me quizzically. 'How much are you earning?' he asked. I told him. 'You'll never earn that teaching,' he insisted. But I was not doing this for the money; I was doing it for me.

I returned to Barrow, determined to get the entry qualifications, and did a crash course with a local Barrow dignitary, Arthur Spencer, a mathematics teacher who had become a headmaster and was an active JP. He had also once been a first-class Rugby League referee, which gave us something in common. His wife, Eleanor, was a teacher, too, and she also helped me to climb my private Everest. Eventually, with much toil and sweat on all our parts I succeeded: I passed the entrance examination! And I wanted to shout it from the topmost tower of Furness Abbey. Barrow allowed me to terminate my contract at the three-quarters stage so that I could begin my course in September 1962. I was about to enter full-time education: it was a momentous thought.

Though I was to return to Rugby League later, first as the driving force behind the beginning of the Student Rugby League and, later still, as a director of Mansfield Marksman, this was the end of my professional career. I was sad to go for there is real comradeship throughout the game of Rugby League and I knew I would miss its warmth. Despite the ferocious high-speed collisions and the physical pounding, after the game, and especially after one's career is over, there is a wonderful friendship and generosity between players and former players. I always feared prop forwards when I first began playing at Hunslet, but scratch below the surface and often there was something of a saint to be found beneath.

Through all the turmoil of those years, at the end of the tunnel of memory, my mind still locks on to three players, who in my mind's eye seem to represent aspects – good and not so good – of the game that became my life for fourteen years or more. First there stands Harry Archer, our stand-off at Workington, crucially injured in that 1958 Cup final against Wigan, later to become a work-mate of mine, and as nice a person as you could hope to meet. As I was an old international with something of a reputation, the opposition would often be told before a match, 'Soften up Darkie Thompson'. A particular game when I was singled out for rough treatment, in fact the one which ended our record of twenty-three games without defeat in 1957-58, was at the Watersheddings, Oldham's ground. Workington were second in the League, Oldham were third. Each one of our games was like a cup final. Each team we played wanted to be the first to end our undefeated run. Two big Oldham forwards tackled me simultaneously while their small scrum-half, Pitchford, stiff-armed me across the face, concussing me and breaking my nose. Our trainer gave me the old cold sponge treatment and I saw Harry looking down at me. I asked him, 'How's my nose?' He replied, 'It's alreet, ma lad. Tha's as 'andsome as ever.' My nose was dreadfully painful but I managed to stumble through the rest of the match. Harry, like the rest of the team, understandably wanted winning money and the cumulative bonus that was due each time we won. There is little compassion among team-mates, even from the likes of Harry, when it comes to shekels.

My second picture is of Brian Edgar, an outstanding international and an extraordinarily gifted player. His swerve had the grace of a bullfighter and he had fantastic speed for a big man. In some matches he appeared super-charged, and his skills made him an automatic choice for the Test selectors. Yet we were never friends. On one occasion, just after he had returned from a tour, he tackled me roughly during training. Jim Brough, the coach, was refereeing. The tackle loosened one of my teeth. When I looked up, Brough and Edgar were smiling at each other. 'Take it easy, Cec,' said Brough. 'You're next,' I replied. But Brough immediately blew his whistle, announced 'End of training' and ran quickly off the field. I was furious. This alliance against me between Edgar and Brough, my second-row partner and team manager respectively, was unforgivable. The next day I had to have two teeth extracted and they were the only ones I lost in the years of professional Rugby League played at the highest level.

My third memory is of another of my remarkable second-row partners. Ted Carroll was a converted winger, only 12½ stone. He was a loyal and intelligent, compassionate person, for whom I had tremendous respect. As a mature family man, I think he had empathy with me, an appreciation of my own reserved nature perhaps. For all that he was 2 stone lighter, he protected me on the field of play. He was a tremendously powerful person and could bowl over with ease 15- or 16-stone forwards. In attack, he could break tackles throwing caution to the wind. He scored numerous solo tries; after one such try, he received a nasty knock close to his eyes which produced a real shiner. Ted characteristically said, 'Ah, but it was worth it, Cec.'

After Ted's playing days were over, his nose was twisted, one part almost horizontal, before it became diagonal. It was so shaped that it could have been used to open corked wine bottles. But there is a positive side to this anecdote: Ted became mine host at the City Varieties public house, named after the famous Leeds television theatre. Performers would call in for a wee dram after and between acts. The shape of Ted's nose attracted the attention of an influential producer and landed Ted many film parts as bookmaker, villain, psychopath, serial killer or rapist. So this gentle man became quite wealthy on the strength of his nose.

PART 3

LEARNING

Chapter 5

There were many factors urging me to become better educated. For a start, the change in my circumstances from raw labourer to the more varied and interesting life I had begun to lead in Workington suggested that my destiny was not yet fixed: my life could be changed if I worked hard enough at it. Another reason was that my two weekly sports articles were giving me an interest in language. Words were food for my intellectual hunger, though I doubt if I would have expressed it quite like that at the time. Whenever I wrote I became oblivious to the outside world; if I was disturbed when I was writing, it was an intrusion. I seemed to stand at the threshold of a new world of learning and longed to be more involved.

My first tentative step had been to take a physiotherapy course, which I did when my divorce was completed. Physiotherapy was something I really enjoyed. I used to have thirty minutes of massage every evening before a home match from a Mr Boult, who was a local artist as well as the town's physiotherapist. After a week of climbing ladders, the massage really relaxed me. It was also a curative of minor injuries. As Mr Boult rubbed and pummelled away my pains he would talk of his interest in painting; it was wonderful to listen to him. Nor was it only his words that moved me. His paintings of the Lake District covered his walls and stirred my senses. There was a touch of true genius about this man, and though I came away from his sessions relaxed in mind and body, his words and paintings made me restless. I was beginning to learn of a world apart from the rough, tough game of Rugby League. Through Mr Boult I began to recognise and appreciate people with developed minds. As well as wanting to keep my body strong and healthy I wanted to learn to enjoy all forms of artistic expression, but it was difficult. 'Cultured' people seemed so far above me, so superior, and I had no idea how, or even if, I could join them. I wanted to fly but found there was lead in my feet, weighing me down.

Because I had been poor I knew the importance of money, but I began to understand too that the true quality of life comes from knowledge and careful reasoning, from creativity and, perhaps above all, from close and generous friendship. I began to visit different churches on Sunday mornings, and took particular pleasure in the informality of the local Presbyterian church. The minister was soft-spoken but his sermons made me think and began to open doors to a different world. And sandwiching these church visits between the Rugby League match on the Saturday and window-cleaning on the Monday seemed to give balance to my faltering steps towards a new life-style.

My former business partner, Stan Thompson, had been content with a dull, tame life; he had his feet firmly on the ground, and had no time for fancy notions. But I was full of ideas. I hated cleaning the windows of houses since so much time was spent chasing payment – sometimes housewives would dodge from room to room making it look as if no one was at home. It seemed to me that if we worked longer hours more business would be created until eventually we could afford to employ other people who would do the manual labour for us. Similarly, if we made more money, more money could be ploughed back into the business: if we got rid of the cart and bought a van we could serve a larger area. I had a vision of us buying one van after another until we covered the whole of Cumbria. But Stan had not been interested. He had enough to suit his interests: the idea of working harder than we already did appalled him.

However, with Stan back in Yorkshire, the first step towards the expansion I wanted was to buy the van I coveted. Jim was sceptical at first, but we were the first mobile window-cleaners in the area and soon even he could see the advantages. The contracts flowed in from factories, hotels, office-blocks and shops until, as I had foreseen, I could afford both to extend my labour force and to give up cleaning house windows.

The money from window-cleaning was enough to live on now that I was on my own, so I used to bank my rugby and media earnings. My bank manager would congratulate me on how my savings were accumulating. In later years, I could look back on his paternal pat on the back with new relish. The heart of capitalism is so simple and yet most people – even some of the most educated people in our society – don't understand the workings of financial institutions.

Banks create credit. Over 90 per cent of all transactions are done by cheque, so a bank needs only a small fraction of their total deposits in the form of cash, just sufficient to meet daily demands from customers. Thus, a deposit of £100 allows £900 worth of credit to be created in the form of overdrafts and loans. The bank now has £1,000 to play with. And when the bank borrows your money from you, in the form of your deposits, it works at one interest rate – say, 10 per cent – but should you borrow from them they charge a higher rate, perhaps 15 per cent. No wonder the banks have such fantastic buildings and make such astonishing profits. Put a few zeros on to the £100s and see how easily money is made. The only risk – as one or two banks have been discovering – is when they lend their money to those who can never pay it back.

Now compare that with somebody who puts in forty-eight hours a week sweating down a pit or in a steel works, or who faces the boredom of an assembly line in a motor assembly plant or a canning factory; ask any factory worker about the tedium of his work, and the damage done to his health, and it is not hard to see that there is injustice in society. But the real injustice is that some are too poorly educated to see what is happening. Nor do you always get the best advice if the bank manager realises that you don't understand banking. My rugby savings were all put into a deposit account, whereas there were many ways in which my money could have been earning me more. My bank manager would greet me each week as I took in my rugby earnings. 'Well done, Mr Thompson, you're building your account up nicely, keep it up!' But I was working for him as well as for me, had I known it.

But I should not complain too much. I was doing all right, and this made people adopt a different attitude towards me. Away from my immediate locality, where it was not known that I was a Rugby League player and a window-cleaner, I found I was treated with a certain deference. I was an exotic, I suppose, a well-dressed black man. For all people knew, I might have been a prince or a president.

Clothes, speech, behaviour and life-style are all part and parcel of the British class-system. I was well dressed and well behaved, but in my own locality I was categorised by my occupation and lack of education. And in Hunslet, for example, ethnic grouping lowered my status too. But the class system is never straightforward. I never encountered racism in Cumbria, and I was accepted because I was an international Rugby League player. Paradoxically, however, the fact that I was a professional rugby player lowered my status elsewhere. The different images presented by Rugby Union and Rugby League, when I was a player, were profound and, although the image of Rugby League has changed over the past two decades, the social stratification remains.

My days were spent, literally and metaphorically, in window gazing. Window-cleaning for a living is a harsh occupation. Ladders have to be moved up and down: you are constantly climbing or carrying. In summer the sun reflects from the glass on to your face and dust adheres to your sweat. In autumn and spring the days are wet, windy, grey, and chilly; winter days are short, with ice, snow and bitter winds. But my mind was kept active with thoughts and ideas. I looked through one set of windows and saw the factory worker, on conveyor belts, involved in the hideous repetitiveness of mass production. I looked through other windows and there were those who stop in hotels, with their smart clothes and smart lives. I didn't know who was happier, but I knew who I wanted to be. And above all it was schools that held my imagination. There my thoughts went wild. Oh, how I wished I could be a pupil in the classroom, to be taught different subjects by qualified teachers. And the most wonderful thing of all for me would have been to find myself transformed, as if by magic, into a teacher myself.

But though my life was changing and new friends, a fast car and even foreign holidays began to be part of my life, I still had a long way to go before I could realise that dream. Certainly I was meeting educated people for the first time, and my tastes had become more sophisticated, but I was still a black Rugby League player with a window-cleaning round.

On the Saturday mornings before away games, when the team would leave the hotel and stroll around the local town, I used to look for bookshops. Since moving to Cumbria I had become fascinated by books. It was the beauty of the Lake District that inspired me to start reading. Once I had seen places like Thirlmere or Rydal Water, Grasmere or Windermere, I found I understood Wordsworth; more than that, having discovered Wordsworth, I found that with his poetry for company it didn't matter where I was, for the beauty of the writing brought the beauty of the Lakes to my mind. And I started to look for other writers whose experiences threw light on my own.

I also began to find that my ambitions were making me a bit of an outsider in Rugby League and that made me uncomfortable. If I no longer felt at ease in that rough, tough world, where on earth did I belong? So I had to accept that I was still just a window-cleaner, on the outside looking in. But sometimes it's the window-cleaner who gets the best view of the house and anyway I knew the present could not go on for ever.

The best view of the house! It was certainly that on one vivid occasion still just as vivid now as it was thirty years ago. I had climbed up to a second-floor window and there I saw a beautiful girl, as in a vision, kneeling naked in a bath. She was about nineteen, a perfect specimen of female beauty, an Aphrodite, a goddess of sensual love. Then in 1994, at the Picasso exhibition at the Tate, at which I spent a whole day with my wife, that vision of thirty years before leapt unbidden into my mind as I stood in front of Picasso's 'Nude with raised arms'. Once again I became completely intoxicated, just as I had been all those years ago, by the symmetry of perfect physical beauty. I longed then, as I do now, to tell all the young people who surround me that life really is full of wondrous things and that those wonders can be grasped, just occasionally, if one tries hard enough.

Chapter 6

It was at this stage in my life that I met Anne – wonderful, patient Anne who has somehow managed to put up with me for all these years. I first met her during the Christmas holidays of 1957. At that time I was going out with a girl called Joyce who was manageress of a gown shop. Joyce seemed very sophisticated to me then: she had her own career, her own money, and even her own car. The first time I took Joyce out we went to a restaurant in Carlisle. At the end of the meal she said, 'I want to pay.' I wouldn't hear of it. 'I can afford it,' I lied. Fortunately she insisted. This was the sort of woman I could like, I decided, and we arranged to go on holiday to Scandinavia together the following summer. And then I met Anne, whom I liked even more.

Anne had just completed a catering course at a college in Leeds but her family came from Workington. Her brother Brian was a Workington Town fan and a friend of mine, and one evening I was invited to join them for a family dinner party at the Lodore Hotel in Borrowdale. Sitting round the table that never-to-be-forgotten evening when my present life began were Anne's father, George Taylor, and her stepmother, Evelyn, Sally Taylor, Anne's aunt, Anne's brother Brian and her best friend, Pauline, a vivacious strawberry blonde with sparkling brown eyes, and myself. George Taylor had invited me but I suspect that it was Brian, my Rugby League friend, who had put him up to it, perhaps in order to leave him free to serenade Pauline. Sadly for him, his strategy misfired. His sister became my wife and Pauline married a college sweetheart in Yorkshire.

Not only was Anne beautiful and handsome in a way that reminded me of my mother, but she was also marvellously well-groomed, kind and sympathetic: the word that sprang to mind when I looked at her was 'decorous'. Naturally, I little realised how quickly my initial admiration of her would become transformed into intense love, but I did know immediately – though she was nineteen and I was thirty-one – that this was someone I wanted to get to know better.

She was also someone I wanted to impress. The meal at the hotel was wonderful, firelight sparkling in the wine glasses, waiters at our beck and call. I was at my best, assured, urbane and happy. But the next time I saw her was the following week, and I was back on my window-cleaning round. I remember it all only too well: I hadn't even bought the van by then and I was wheeling my barrow in the sleet when I saw a car I recognised. It was Anne's father's car, and worse still, Anne was in it. I could not bear to let her see me in my working-clothes, looking no more than a common labourer, which is what I was, and I hid in the ditch as they passed.

Yet I must have made an impression on her because when she went back to the West Riding we continued to keep in touch by letter. I thought it possible that Anne and I were falling in love, but I knew that the real test would come when I went on my Scandinavian holiday with Joyce. Would Anne stay loyal to me though I was away with another woman? Would I stay loyal to Anne? As it happened – to Joyce's chagrin, I suppose – I never stopped thinking about Anne, and on the boat home between Esbjerg in Denmark and Newcastle I wrote her a six-page letter. It touches me to think that she has still kept it; indeed she has kept all the letters I have ever written her.

But there were problems. At first I felt alien amongst Anne's family and friends. My skin pigmentation had caused me some problems down the years though, thanks to my rugby prowess and the fact that I lived for most of my mature years in Cumbria where racial problems are practically non-existent, I was generally more confused than anxious about my colour. Now I worried whether Anne would see through my wafer-thin confidence and tire of me. Perhaps I was just a passing exotic fancy of hers? But I soon discovered, to my considerable surprise, as I moved from person to person among her family and friends, that I was actually becoming quite an interesting person to them. I opened up to the people I liked and found that my trust was reciprocated. It was not long before genuine relationships developed and this was truly a revelation to me. Gradually self-doubt was being eroded and self-respect emerged.

So those first few months with Anne are undoubtedly the most important period of my life. She was vastly more assured than me, but warm and caring and generous with her love, as she has remained throughout our marriage. Totally lacking in confidence, I had become extrovert to the point of being brash. And I was still a working-class black man, a manual worker, divorced and twelve years her senior. But for the first time I could see the outline of wider horizons, hitherto totally unattainable, which perhaps I could just reach out for with her help.

There were other problems too. I really wanted to win the approval of Anne's family. Fortunately they not only gave me another incentive to improve myself, but also provided the means. Anne's aunt, Sally, was deputy head of a large school in Whitehaven, and I took to her immediately, partly because she was so well read and well informed on so many subjects, but mostly, I suspect, simply because of the sheer number of books she possessed. Initially, at least, Sally was not so keen on me. She was fiercely protective of Anne, and clearly I was not an ideal suitor. I don't think it was my colour that worried her: it was just me. She constantly warned Anne not to fall in love with me in case I let her down. Even after Anne and I were married, Sally worried that the relationship would not last. Yet, as time wore on, I must have won Sally over, and she started to take a genuine interest in me.

Indeed, Sally's influence on me was vast. For the first time I was given real assistance with my education. She helped me with the rudiments of the English language, and the books she lent me broadened my reading tremendously. She was lovely to look at, with rosy cheeks and an intelligent face, although she could also be cantankerous and stubborn. Though she had no personal worries about my pigmentation, she was all too well aware that not everyone would be so broad-minded, and warned us of the dangers. Nor was her help only theoretical. By living frugally she had put aside quite a lot of money. When she died, we found that she had so arranged her affairs that our son Mark would never have to cope with being as poor as I had been. However, that was in the future. For the present we were in love, Anne and I: we could cope with the way others looked at us because we were secure in one another. And so we got engaged.

Anne's parents were divorced. Her stepfather was a racist who banned me from the house, but the rest of her family could not have been more supportive. Her father George was a rugby enthusiast, like his son a Workington Town fan, who welcomed me with open arms. In fact, George was a man of many parts: he was on both the borough and county councils, he was an avid reader, particularly of philosophy, and a keen golfer. And his second wife was a county player.

My relationship with Anne broadened my life in a hundred ways, some of which were totally unexpected. I loved the Lake District from the moment I first saw it and often went fell-walking but, though I had admired the climbers I had seen, I had never thought to join them. In fact, I saw it as next to lunacy. However, the fiancé of Anne's half-sister Pat, Harold Martin, explained that if you use an intelligent approach to rock-climbing you can minimise the danger almost to zero, especially at the grades of climbing he pursued. Moreover, he seemed a placid, sensible chap – not a lunatic at all – and so Anne and I gave it a try. Our first climb was in a Borrowdale valley near Keswick. Climbing is the only way really to appreciate the beauty of the Lake District, because it both gets you out of the crowds and lifts you up to become part of those noble panoramas. We loved every minute of that first climb, joined a club, and for years continued to glory in those vistas.

So, engaged to Anne and petrified by the dangers ahead, my life as a student began as I started to work for those 'O' and 'A' levels at Huddersfield. I put my beautiful MG sports car into an auction market, accepting whatever price was offered, and spent the summer of 1962 in the Leeds City reference library preparing for my studies. I wasn't eligible for a grant, but I hoped my window-cleaning business would provide the necessary cash; to this end I had already arranged that Jim should become a partner, much to his delight. 'Thanks, Cec!' he enthused. 'I'll never let you down!' My only conditions were that I should be paid a standing order of £3 per week, and that I would work in the business during vacations to make a little extra money for myself. 'This is all very generous of you, Cec,' Jim told me as we shook hands on the deal. 'I don't see how I can ever repay you.'

The standing order looked after my bedsitter in Huddersfield. It was absolutely essential to keep my costs to a minimum if my plans were going to work out, because I had no idea how long it would take me to qualify. For the first time for a long time I was forced to be parsimonious, and Anne and I decided to postpone our wedding at least until I had obtained the 'O' levels I was after.

As often as possible Anne used to drive me back to Cumbria. I was still something of a local hero: I enjoyed the break from work, and the attention. I was regularly invited to youth clubs, which gave me the satisfying feeling that I was wanted and that I could still be of some benefit to the community. The youngsters seemed genuinely inspired by my presence and involvement. To watch a lad in a wheelchair forget his handicap as he concentrated on winning a game of table tennis, and then to see the look of triumph when he won, always left me feeling chuffed.

However, my day-to-day life in Huddersfield was less immediately rewarding. My diet consisted of coffee for breakfast, a pork pie for lunch, and a college-subsidised meal in the evening; the rest of my time was spent in study. It was a monastic existence, but it was the only way I was going to make it through the quagmire of examinations and deadlines. My consolations were Anne's love, my dreams for the future, and my regular income from the business. And then, early in my second term, Jim wrote to me: my van and ladders were to be found in Workington; he had set up business on his own. Not only had Jim told most of our best customers that I had left the area for good, but, even more damagingly, he had submitted new tenders to the local education authorities for cleaning school windows for the coming year, showing prices a good deal lower than those that he and I had put down on the tenders we had submitted. I had always believed that if I were kind to others then others would be kind to me. Jim proved me wrong.

He had stolen my present finances from me, which was bad enough, but he had also stolen a large chunk of my past, and was even threatening my future. I had worked tirelessly to build up that business. I had invested my strength and my reputation in it, climbing ladders though every bone ached from the rugby, charming clients though all I really wanted was to read or rest, going out in all weathers though I was desperate to keep warm, and now I had almost nothing to show for it. I felt trapped in Huddersfield, penned in by my studies and my new poverty.

Anne, of course, was wonderful, and used her salary to support us while I tried to salvage something from the mess. Only two contracts had not been destroyed by Jim's cunning. Every Friday evening I borrowed Anne's car and travelled to Cumbria; every Sunday I returned to my studies. It is always essential to invest in a business to get a real return: I took on Dennis Williamson, an ex-rugby colleague, paying him from my diminishing savings because I no longer had an income. In business it is true that time is money, and because I had so little money I had to invest all the time I could. It was necessary to work late in my search for new customers. One evening I saw a hotel with filthy windows. I asked the proprietor, 'Could we clean your windows?' He replied, 'Certainly.' Williamson and I made an excellent job of it, hoping to get a regular order. When we finished I asked if we could have dinner for two. He said, 'You sure can, we have a fine menu.' The meal cost more than we made cleaning the windows, but it was all part of my strategy for getting business: investing in order to accumulate. However, even the best laid plans can go astray. 'Business is slack at the moment,' the proprietor told me. 'But I'll let you know if I want the windows cleaning again.' I'm still waiting.

I was working to a punishing routine. Driving back to Huddersfield I used to leave the windows of the car open, letting the icy winds keep me conscious, and sometimes I had to take forty winks at the roadside. Fortunately I still had friends and many people allowed me credit, especially when I explained my position.

Barclays Bank were particularly helpful. I had invested a proportion of my Rugby League earnings in endowment policies throughout my career. It is quite common in cases like mine for financial institutions to pressurise businesses and private depositors, forcing them to surrender such policies – at less than their value – to raise needed cash. It is easy to see why the financial institution should be eager to take the policy on, as it earns annual profits. If, for example, you surrender a twenty-year policy at ten years of its life the bank gets the profit on the first ten years that is the right of the holder, and therefore the compound profit for holding it for twenty years though it only holds it for ten. Yet I endured no such pressures from Barclays. Jim had stolen nearly everything I possessed but the goodwill remained so, despite everything, I carried on with my education.

But now other, much more serious, problems arose. Dreadful scenes sometimes erupted between Anne and me. As I began to struggle through my 'O' and 'A' levels, I began to think that anyone who was not 'graduate material', as I now imagined myself to be, was somehow of less consequence than me. Of course this was quite appallingly arrogant. Because I was now in the process of becoming more formally educated than Anne, attending lectures and tutorials and engaged in constant study, I found that my thinking was far sharper than hers. I tended to grow impatient if she did not discuss a problem, as I thought, 'rationally'.

Of course Anne's busy working life allowed her little time for the sort of cultural activities, or indulgences, which I now drank in. But that was no reason for me to consider myself some kind of superior being. As I struggled towards my 'O' levels Anne had been appointed school meals organiser for the West Riding county council, and was living in Dewsbury. This was an important job, with responsibility for all aspects of the schools' kitchens and kitchen equipment in her area, for the appointment and training of all kitchen staff, for balancing their budgets and for liaison between the local county authorities, directors of education and the school governors. And, even more important, she was responsible for the variety and nutritional value of all school meals.

How could I have become so selfish and so arrogant in my attitude towards Anne? Never at a loss for words, I was well on my way to becoming a pretentious smart alec. Anne had graduated from being a catering student to become a greenhorn worker with considerable responsibilities and along the way had encountered a streetwise window-cleaner who was trying to become a student. Did the disputes occur because I found Anne's changed status difficult to live with? Was I, perhaps, simply jealous of her and her achievements?

Our values and aspirations were certainly changing and there were other issues of a more intimate nature. I would be mentally and physically exhausted at the end of a day, and Anne grew increasingly frustrated by my listlessness. Tensions built up for which I was wholly to blame. Anne had tolerated many of my social shortcomings: on many occasions she would comment quietly on some *faux pas* I had committed, hoping to save embarrassment all round, but succeeding only in piercing my pride. If I guffawed, Anne would suggest that I laughed in a more dignified manner: there would be a little nudge and I would be told 'Don't be so loud'. There would be comments about the colour combinations of my clothes or a suggestion that I had been insufficiently careful with my shaving. Only now do I realise how dreadfully self-centred I had become, and but for Anne's patience our relationship could have been seriously endangered.

Jim's timing had been exquisite. On top of everything else, that winter of 1963–64 was among the most severe of the century. Imagine what it was like on top of ladders, dipping hands into pails of freezing water. In Huddersfield, lighting a fire meant carrying coal up three floors, so I simply borrowed an electric fire from Cumbria. Unfortunately this sent my landlady's electricity bill sky high, as I discovered one day when she was standing outside my door. 'Enough's enough, Mr Thompson,' she said, arms folded across her chest. 'You can get out now!' I was desperate to placate her. 'I'm awfully sorry, Mrs Gledhill. Look, please accept an open cheque.' I couldn't afford the money but couldn't face being homeless.

This only worsened my desperate financial situation of course. Despite my best efforts, the cost of books, exams and accommodation was eating away my savings and, though I was surviving, it was precarious. One devastating result of Jim's treachery was that, because my funds had been so badly eroded, I had to squash the four-year course into three years. Maths was a torture, and quadratic equations gave me nightmares. The staff always claimed that if we had problems of any kind they were always available to help us. I took my problems to the head of department, an Oxford graduate. To begin with he was sympathetic, and tried several times to explain what was quite simple to him; eventually, though, he realised his technique was not working. Finally, in exasperation, he told me, 'If you don't understand that, then you've no right to be in this college.' I almost wilted under such a direct assault: had I done so my life would have taken a very different direction. However, I persevered, quadratic equations and all, and at the end of the first year obtained five 'O' levels.

In the second year, 1963–64, I did two more 'O' levels and began my 'A' level courses. But my German 'O' level was causing serious problems. I had holidayed in Austria, and visited Germany three times, so I chose German as my foreign language. What idiocy! I had no notion how difficult the German language would be to speak and to write. The lack of logic about gender annoyed me particularly; surely *das Mädchen* ought to be feminine, yet there it is, large as life, neuter. Even simple things, such as the capital letter for every noun, needed great concentration; comprehension was right out of the window. I had to take the exam four times, with two different boards, before passing.

However, my blind desire to improve myself, egged on by pride, persisted. I could not bring myself to use foul language or be roused to anger. Politeness and consideration for others prevailed together with a bizarre, absolutely obsessive preoccupation with personal hygiene. Were these attributes the benefit of my orphanage upbringing? If so, there were at least some positives for Anne to build on, I thought, though our constant disagreements continued.

At first our love was intense, almost intoxicating. Then came the hideous cut-off point when my studies became the only area of importance in my life. I had crossed the Rubicon. There was no turning back. My mind had to triumph over my heart. This turning point must have caused Anne deep distress but I was too egocentric then to be too much concerned. I had already made too many sacrifices: now I was rigid in my determination to exclude everything but study.

It is a fact that Anne would have left me then to return to her mother had she had a stable home. Furthermore, her mother had persistently warned her that our marriage would be shortlived if she insisted on marrying a working-class black man. Her half-brother predicted that I would not be able to support her in her proper life-style since I was just a window-cleaner. Of course this sort of talk and attitude inflamed Anne and so she was determined to stand rocklike beside me. And for that I shall thank her to my dying day.

Chapter 7

Our wedding, so long postponed, was fixed at last for August 8 1964, that is, at the end of my second year at Huddersfield. With typical generosity Sally covered the costs but naturally Anne wanted me to help organise and rehearse the wedding. Unfortunately, the only available opportunity was the Whitsun holiday which, as any student knows, falls just before the examination period, and I refused to waste any revision time.

I was learning a lot just then. For instance, I had always thought Anne beautifully sweet natured. 'Do your exams come before our wedding?' she shouted at me.

'I'm afraid they do,' I answered.

'Right! That's it!' She stormed away, and I thought I would never see her again.

Yet somehow we got things straightened out, and the wedding was on again. I looked through the local press for somewhere to live when we were married: our first home. I rang up about flats. My accent and name caused no problems on the phone but, when I arrived in person and said who I was I was told, 'I'm sorry, Mr Thompson, the room has been taken since you called.'

I wasn't surprised. Even in my rugby days I'd had problems in Huddersfield. When I was with Barrow I used to travel by car behind the team coach. One day Barrow were playing Huddersfield away and I had plans to lure Geoff Gunney, a player I admired, to join us from Hunslet; I was going to stay overnight at my sister's home in Leeds. But my plans got scuppered when Bill Burgess swallowed his tongue and almost died on the field. He was taken to hospital; I stayed with him until it was clear that he would recover, and then, as it was late, looked for somewhere to stay nearby. Curiously, it seemed that all the hotels were full. Even the George, the birthplace of Rugby League and the best hotel in Huddersfield, had no room for me that night. There was nothing to be gained by arguing, by pointing out that they still had rooms enough for any white man who wanted one. There was more dignity in just walking away. But, as a legacy from that time, whenever I am refused a request I wonder whether the answer would have been the same had I been white.

I determined that no bigotry would spoil our wedding. I had not met many of Anne's family: her divorced parents had both remarried so there were a lot of them to meet. I had crossed swords with Anne's stepfather, however: his hatred of me was so intense that, one bitterly cold winter, he had ordered Anne from his house on my account. An aunt took her in. It was a relief to find the rest of his family didn't share his feelings.

It was also a relief that he didn't come to our wedding. I can't say I missed him, and everyone who was there had a wonderful time. Apart from Anne's family there was my cousin Joan from Canada, several of the staff from my college, and of course Gus Risman and his family. It was a magnificent day, followed by a delightful sunny honeymoon in North Wales and Anglesey.

We returned to live in a third-floor flat, almost an attic, in an old Victorian terraced house on Imperial Road in the Edgerton district of Huddersfield. It was a well furnished, spacious flat, with an open-plan sitting-room, a dining-room, a small bedroom, a kitchen and a sun-trap balcony. We both thought it was gorgeous.

However, I could not afford to let up on my regime. I had passed my exams that summer but still had another year to go. I became utterly single-minded. People who had known me in my playing days sometimes contacted me; frequently I was asked to play golf, a favourite game of retired sportsmen, and hypocritically I would take their telephone numbers, saying that I would phone back. I never did: I would not let anything destroy my concentration. I never involved myself in any sport during those three long years, and never went to the cinema or watched television. The only exception to this was when Anne once, just once, demanded that I take her to see Julie Andrews in *The Sound of Music*. On that single occasion, knowing that to do otherwise would mean a premature end to our wonderful marriage, I acquiesced.

Otherwise I am afraid Anne had little social life. Every day she prepared the meals and did the housework and then each morning she had to drive fifteen miles or so to the Dewsbury, Batley, Morley or Spen Valley area, wherever she was to spend the day. Always she subjected herself to my needs and, smiling and diplomatic, stood silently in the background, never failing to give me the moral and practical support I needed. Each morning, always dissatisfied with my previous evening's lecture preparation, constantly frustrated by my essays, always flustered, totally ill-prepared for the day, I had a 200-yards sprint to the bus stop followed by a ten-minute journey which allowed me to walk calmly into college for my day's studies.

As always, we were desperately short of money, and I simply had to go to Cumbria during the Christmas vacation that year to earn something from cleaning windows. Life was quite cosy in Huddersfield: our flat was warm as were the rooms in college. But on top of my ladder I was exposed to the fierce, icy winds from the Atlantic and from Siberia to the east. At times I worked with my fists alternately clenched in my trouser-pocket to keep frostbite at bay. I would pray that some customer would know me and ask me indoors for a cup of tea. I don't believe in wishing parts of my life away but I desperately wanted those Christmas days to pass as quickly as possible. It was devastatingly cold, with violent storms; I suffered waking nightmares, desperate for the end of the day. Sometimes I would be rain-soaked; at others exposed to those dreadful winds which bit into my body and even into my mind. There were times when I seemed barely to exist; the cold had penetrated my entire being and the discomfort did not allow rational thinking. I said to myself, 'If I do get through this dreadful period of my life, and someone says to me "Aren't you lucky", I will happily strangle them.'

It was a little later in that third and last year, as I struggled for my 'A' levels, that I suffered some sort of nervous breakdown. It was as though I had become almost literally dehumanised. And if I became human again, I thought, I would make no progress towards my goal. In those awful days everything I touched seemed suddenly to fly out of control: my reading, the essay I was preparing, the simplest domestic arrangements. Then I would panic, shaken by hysteria. I would imagine myself submerged by financial pressures, or persecuted by my bank manager. I would have a run of poor essay marks and my confidence would vanish completely. And those terrible disputes with Anne would continue day after day.

I persuaded myself that I must be on the verge of madness. I must regain my composure at all costs. Had I completely miscalculated the price of self-advancement? By turns my behaviour was totally erratic: sometimes it was exaggeratedly flamboyant, at other times I used to creep in terror about the corridors, clutching my anxieties to my chest. I was terrified of letting the outside world think I had made a mistake – which I felt sure I had – in trying to change the course of my life in midstream. I saw myself as just a fool, a buffoon. I was beginning to loathe myself.

I shared none of this suffering with Anne. Why I do not know except, I suppose, that if I had stopped to talk, I would have fallen even further behind with the terrible pressure of my studies. She never saw much of me at that time anyway, and I regarded myself as too tough to seek consolation even for a moment, even from my own wife. I was in an appalling Catch-22 situation. There seemed to be no escape, only that dreadful daily round of obsessive anxiety and irrational self-analysis.

Anne had met me in 1957 as a carefree, amiable fellow: something about me must have attracted her. Now that amiable man had grown into a tortured, harassed being after she had married him in the elementary stages of a six-year stint of full-time education. Yet somehow she stayed by me.

Then for no good reason, or for no good reason that my conscious mind could understand, but to my intense relief, the dark shadows gradually began to steal away and the days to be touched again with happiness. New ideas, new insights began again to fill my mind, now apparently refreshed, certainly calmer. And that new knowledge bred new attainments. But there were frustrations, too, for the more knowledge I acquired, the deeper seemed the jungle of my ignorance.

In that last year maths too got a bit easier when Mr Wilson, my maths lecturer, took me under his wing. Our friendship survived my time at Huddersfield, and when I first started at Leeds University he let Anne and me stay in his house until we found accommodation of our own. Another lecturer, Gordon Craven, helped me with German language. In fact, I got private tuition from various lecturers free of charge; they knew my circumstances and showed their sympathy: they joined the multitude of people who have helped or influenced me at vital times in my life, more than I can ever manage to thank or repay.

One speech day at Huddersfield I was awarded the History prize. That was my proudest day. At last I began to feel free; education had loosened the shackles of my upbringing. And then another door opened when, towards the end of my course, Michael Mollan, the director of studies, took me to one side and suggested I should definitely apply for a university place.

It was a breathtaking notion. Originally, I had imagined trying to get into a PE college or to be a school sportsmaster. A place at university had really been miles beyond my dreams but, as I have done for most of my adult life, I followed my intuition.

Unfortunately, filling in the UCCA form was as hard as trying to tackle another 'A' level. I have always hated any kind of form filling, and this was dreadful. I had to cover all my employment since I had left school twenty-two years earlier, put down school examinations taken, results, activities, hobbies, background information about myself, education from the age of eleven, and do it in such a way that I appeared a likely university candidate.

I also had to justify why I wanted to read economics. Perhaps the fact that I ran my own business helped because, to my astonishment, I was invited for interview at Leeds University.

If I had been nervous going to Huddersfield for an interview you can imagine what I was like going to Leeds. I had spent the previous weeks reading the *Economist* and the *Financial Times*: it did no good because everything I had ever learned seeped out of me. So did everything I had ever drunk – I went to the toilet five times in as many minutes. And, though I did not drink alcohol, I still developed DTs.

I had chosen Leeds deliberately because I was known in the city and have always thought of myself as a true son of Leeds. I was conceived in Leeds. My father had in part decorated the Leeds Town Hall. Both my parents are buried in Leeds and my sister, Linda, was cremated there. Before she died she and her husband ran a flourishing confectionery business there. My brother Bob lives in Leeds and once worked there as a cobbler before going down the mines. My mother and her second husband ran a successful bakery and confectionery business in Leeds. I grew up in Leeds and played professional rugby in Leeds for Hunslet. Then, in the years that followed, after university, I was nurtured by the warmth and generosity of the Lord Mayor of Leeds, Ronnie Feldman, and his wife, and of the Jewish community generally, with whom I have an instinctive sympathy and have always felt at home. On one occasion the Feldmans even laid on a civic reception for me, to which I was allowed to invite a dozen or more of my friends. I came to believe that Leeds had adopted me, was supporting me, and had even become my guardian angel.

'Sit down, Mr Thompson,' the interviewer said. 'Would you like a cup of coffee? Now, tell me, what was it like playing at Wembley?' I could answer that one. In fact, I could answer all the board's questions. They asked me a lot about rugby, very little about economics, and finally said, 'Mr Thompson, we will welcome you at this university if you get the necessary qualifications.' Once I had taken this in I was relieved, but apprehensive. Would I be able to cope, or had my dreams taken me right out of my depth? Behind the jubilation was doubt.

It was a summer of suspense. Not only did I have my 'A' levels to contend with: I was still fighting the impenetrable *der, die* and *das* of the German language. While I awaited my results my business won a lucrative month's contract with the local British Steel Corporation, and by working round the clock we made enough money to allow Anne and me a well deserved holiday abroad. The holiday was wonderful, a chance to escape my worries, but when we got back there was a letter on the mat. I opened it, trying not to be too eager in case the news was bad, and read my results, twice. It seemed impossible to believe, but I had qualified for a three-year honours degree course in economics with philosophy as my supplementary subject in the first year.

Chapter 8

I started university in October 1965. It was like going into outer space, falling into one of Professor Hawking's black holes. I had no idea what preparations I should make: the only thing I could think of was to buy pens and paper.

Anne and I had moved into a modern maisonette in a peaceful cul-de-sac in Morley: it had a comfortable drawing-room, two bedrooms, a kitchen and bathroom. It was perfect, and of course Anne was now living within her main working area. Morley is on the periphery of Leeds, about six miles from the university, a small textile town with a population of about 44,000. It had, still has, a Victorian look about it with its imposing town hall and terraced houses. I used to catch a bus on the Leeds side of Morley, not far from the Leeds United football ground at Elland Road. St Peter's Crescent, where we lived, was on top of a hill overlooking the ground and on match days supporters' cars used to be parked as far from the ground as Morley.

At the end of our crescent stood St Peter's church and my bus stop for Leeds. Opposite the bus stop was a pub; indeed there were two pubs within twenty yards of each other. Perhaps I entered them at the most eight times in the four years I was at university, so austere was my social life.

Almost immediately I allowed myself to be caught up in a whirlpool of lectures, tutorials, seminars, lecture notes, essays. At the end of the day I would be at the Pack Horse, a pub opposite the university, at 9.00 p.m. for a relaxed, humorous half-hour with my new friends Terry Swift, David Thompson and Joe Bradshaw (of whom more later), all mature students from the economics and sociology departments; then Anne would call to take me home. Saturdays I spent in the Leeds City reference library; on Sundays I studied at home. I could

keep up with current economic affairs in newspapers and journals at
the Brotherton library in the university – but by and large the swinging
1960s passed me by. This new routine was dragging me away from all
contact with my previous life. When I returned to window-cleaning
in the vacations, my talk seemed artificial. I did not socialise, I simply
played the fool. Was I happy? I don't know. All I do know is that I
stood between two cultures and that I belonged to neither.

Anne has always had a gift for organising marvellous dinner parties,
and whenever we could we entertained my friends and hers in our
maisonette. Anne played golf and tennis with friends, won trophies,
and even attended evening classes to pass 'O' and 'A' level courses and
to qualify as a teacher. So, for a change, it was not exactly all work
and no play any longer, especially during my second year when I had
Student Rugby League to look after.

However, for a long time I really had little sense of being in control
of my life. I suppose in a way it was a return to childhood, perhaps
even to the childhood I had been denied. Certainly I found no shortage
of potential surrogate fathers: Professor Maurice Beresford was head of
the humanities faculty; my personal tutor was John Brothwell; others
were George Rainee, Professor Roy Wilkinson and Ken Woolmer.
These were wonderful people and they all worked hard to put me at
my ease. Anne and I went to each of their houses for a meal, and the
conversation always seemed to revolve around my life history. It
astonished me – and still does – to realise the respect these intellectuals
seemed to have for my eccentric achievements. Yet here was George
Rainee, admittedly a devoted Leeds Rugby League supporter, discussing
my progression from orphanage to university as if it were part of some
grand design! I had certainly chosen the right university. After all, the
city of Leeds boasted three professional Rugby League clubs, Bramley,
Hunslet and Leeds, and at the time three renowned Rugby Union
clubs, Headingley, Morley and Roundhay.

I thank the stars I had my rugby background, the support of my
tutors, and above all the support of Anne, because without them I
would surely never have survived. The affair with Jim had left me

financially naked, and a combination of physical exhaustion and anxiety as I tried to repair the damage had brought me to the edge of a mental breakdown. And now I was at university, which intensified the pressure.

My sensations were odd. I felt not only inadequate but also conspicuous – like some sort of primitive single-cell creature under the microscope, something that might be observed with interest but could never be accepted as an equal. Not only were the academics demonstrably smarter than me, but even my fellow students seemed to leave me standing. They all appeared to have the capacity to soak up the lecture material and combine their learning with a hectic social life. For me lectures were utter confusion and it took me so long to get my lecture notes sorted out that there was never any time to go out. This was hardly fun for Anne.

In fact, I don't suppose any of it was much fun for Anne. I must have been hard to live with, for I tended to take my anxieties home with me, and at the same time she was using her salary – and did so for seven full years – to keep us both. I got an education, a host of new experiences and a series of new friends. Anne simply got a continuously rising overdraft. Yet she stayed with me, and gradually we learned to relax with each other and to enjoy each other's company, and at last I learned how utterly impossible I had been to live with.

My new friends were important too. One was Joe Bradshaw. An affluent former estate agent in his late forties, Joe had decided to sit for a degree in sociology as a mature student. His impeccable grooming stood out like a beacon among the unkempt students. His manner, too, set him apart. He was a committed socialist with an expensive car, and he was bursting with nervous energy and wry humour. I felt dwarfed in his company.

I met him in the Students' Union during the first week of the course. His hair was greying, which was reassuring among the beatniks. 'What brought you to university?' I asked.

'Call me Joe,' he said, putting my question to one side. 'What's your name?'

'Cec Thompson,' I replied.

'Okay, Cec, now sit back and listen. Once upon a time I used to be the ragged trousered philanthropist – have you read that book? Pity! Anyway, there I was trying to prevent my fellow workers, the proletariat, from being exploited by their bosses, the bourgeoisie.'

This is heavy stuff, I thought: I must have a look at the book. Joe continued. 'But I didn't want to be a martyr; I wasn't prepared to sacrifice my life for my countrymen.' So these are the sort of topics that get discussed in the humanities faculty! 'I'd become a convener in a large factory after I'd qualified as an engineer, and I was union secretary for a while, and then suddenly I had to be rushed into hospital for an operation on an ulcer. I tell you, Cec, I thought my life had come to end, and it occurred to me that if I did survive I was blowed if I was going to devote it all to others. It was time I put family first. 'So what does a left winger do to join the capitalist system? I opened a small office behind Leeds Town Hall and started business as an estate agent. In no time at all I had a very profitable little concern. But one day, over lunch in the Victoria Hotel, I met a friend, Harry Newton, a WEA lecturer, and he nagged me into getting some qualifications. So I sold my business, invested the proceeds, and here I am.'

Years later I met Joe again and once again we sat together in the Students' Union. He was his usual talkative self. 'You know, Cec, I wasted three long years studying sociology in this place. I'm telling you, the staff in the sociology department were the silliest people I've ever met before or since. I had been told not to offend the staff if I wanted a good degree, but there are limits. So I bloody well did open my mouth, and I did get a poor degree.'

Joe went on to join the prison service as a visiting sociology teacher and wrote a number of very successful books and pamphlets to help uneducated people to understand, for example, the complexities of buying a house and in other ways to help to steer them through the everyday difficulties of life without having to spend hundreds of pounds on expensive lawyers.

Another mature student, Terry Swift, an ardent fan, indeed the administrator, of Batley Rugby League club, soon became my best friend. He was in his mid-twenties and took his studies in his stride, while I had to struggle from the start. Without Terry the nightmare of lectures would have finished me, I'm sure. I never did get the hang of taking notes while trying to understand what the lecturers were talking about. After a few weeks of agony – my writing became illegible when I tried to write at the speed required – Terry took pity on me, and though I had to sacrifice sport on Wednesday afternoons to copy Terry's notes from the previous week's lectures, at least I now knew what was going on.

Terry is director of business studies at a tertiary college now, and when we meet we talk about the old times, and what motivated us to go to university at all. For those who go directly from school, university seems the most natural thing in the world, simply a continuation of an existing situation. But the stories mature students have to tell are always much more varied, more interesting, more vivid. 'I was twenty-one,' said Terry, 'and I was in a rut. I was a civil servant but I'd no real qualifications, no sixth-form education or degree, and the next step for promotion was an interview at the age of twenty-seven, which was an eternity away. I've got to do something about this, I thought, so I took three 'A' levels in one year, got good results, and tried my luck by applying to Leeds University. The rest is history.'

'So how did you live?'

'God knows! I got leave without pay.'

'Was it worth it?'

'It certainly helped to bring me out of myself, meeting people from different backgrounds, from comprehensive and public schools, from Barnsley to Botswana. The experience was great and I enjoyed everything, the studies and the social life. But whether it was worth it financially I don't know. A university qualification isn't a licence to print money. I didn't want to spend three years training my brain to go through hoops just to end up in some stultifying job at ICI or Unilever: I expect they make more money but I couldn't see myself worrying over the next soap powder development.'

'It sounds like you've got reservations.'

'No. Not really. I don't measure success in money. University gave me freedom, freedom to learn for myself, and that's given me the freedom to help others to learn. These days I look at both sides of the question before I vote Labour.'

I certainly count myself among those Terry helped, but even with his assistance I still had to work harder than ever. My university days were the best of times and the worst of times. I had a wife but no life with her. I was as poor as a church mouse, and totally dependent on Anne. I was working my fingers to the bone. Nor did my degree make my fortune – I have always made more money from my window-cleaning business. Yet I have even fewer reservations than Terry. University changed my life, broadening my horizons in ways inconceivable before I began my studies.

Sometimes when Workington played Leeds at Headingley I would come across Cumbrians who recognised me. I used to take them into the university and show them around like an excited kid with a new toy. It is a strange thought that there are millions in this country who have never seen inside a university campus. I felt thrilled to show them around. I would take them into the Students' Union, buy them a drink at the bar, and let them see how their taxes got spent. In many ways I felt as out of place as my Cumbrian guests, incredulous at the leisurely pace of university life and the students' easy assumption of privilege. I was pleased by my friends' reaction. There were times I thought I was the only one who found university life extraordinary. Yet there was never any envy. 'Thanks, Cec,' they said. 'If we'd not met you, we'd not have seen this unbelievable place. It does not matter so much about the match now; you've helped to make it a marvellous weekend, absolutely fantastic!' They had merely been shown round a few buildings: what if they attended a full degree course?

The fact is that only a tiny minority of people know the benefits of education and motivate their children to study. Perhaps this is because the real rewards of education are intangible rather than financial, or because for most people the time they are expected to study hardest is the very time, the teens, when they want to do it least. But I do know this: I have cleaned windows, and I have been to university, and I have no doubt at all which I preferred, and which I want for my son. Manual labour does not make you a better person: at best it gives one an appreciation of the alternatives, but more often it deadens the spirit and dulls the mind. I was poor as a student, and amassing further debts which would stay with me for many years. For example, I knew that when I eventually qualified I would have to pay off seven years' National Insurance contributions for the time I had been a full-time student. But I was amassing other things as well, knowledge, experience and friendships that broadened my life beyond measure.

When I entered the university in October 1965 there was one friendship I certainly couldn't have predicted. Professor Maurice Beresford, economic historian, was the chairman of the school of economics and head of the humanities faculty. He was very much the Goliath of the department, and I wasn't even a David. His was a commanding figure, and his stentorian upper-middle-class voice told all who heard him that he also had the upper hand.

Meeting him for the first time was traumatic. His reputation for possessing a razor-sharp mind and for real intellectual rigour seemed amply justified by his demeanour. I murmured to myself, 'Well, Cec, how are you going to survive three years of this guy?' The best advice I could give myself was to keep out of his way as much as possible. It was a good idea, but inappropriate: I was to encounter him every other week in his tutorials. They were like inquisitions, his perceptive questions demanding intelligent and accurate answers. Yet I learned to enjoy them: they were certainly lively affairs, peppered with his witticisms and regulated by his sharp mind. His enthusiasm was infectious too.

Several of his books were on our reading list, in particular *The Lost Villages of England* and *New Towns of the Middle Ages*. We were aware that he had won an outstanding reputation as an historian. In contrast, there I was. I soon realised that he would not endure fools gladly. He was strictly teetotal and, worse, a non-sportsman, so what chance had

I got, a thick working–class rugby player of the type known for spending hours gulping pints of ale while singing vulgar songs and wenching?

Yet MB was a better man than I had allowed, with a remarkable range of sympathy and interests; he was immensely good company and fully at ease with an extraordinary variety of people, including me. So though some considered him an intellectual snob, I came to recognise that he valued the plain and the genuine as much as the rarefied atmosphere of culture and scholarship. He was the dominant personality of the university. He had taught there for most of his life, thirty-five years in all, and had always been active beyond its walls as well.

In particular, MB spent a great deal of time helping at an approved school, Eastmoor. He took groups from Eastmoor to the university mountain hut in the Dudden Valley in the middle of the Lake District, helped by students chosen, I suspect, because they could provide transport. Anne and I often joined these weekends, my speciality being to take the boys along Striding Edge and Swirral Edge. Those days were of special therapeutic value to the boys and gave the students a valuable insight into a particular stratum of society; they also gradually closed the social gap between Beresford and myself. But, perhaps, most important of all, I noted the endless patience he had with the sincerely simple, in complete contrast to the impatience he showed to self-important mediocrities.

Every Wednesday, in the late morning, an economics student had to give a lecture about some aspect of the country's economy. When it came to my turn, I had two weeks in which to prepare. From that moment stage fright set in, causing Anne two weeks of suffering. I became totally neurotic. When the day came to give the lecture, my hands grew cold and damp, my legs felt like rubber tubes, waves of nausea swept over me. I told myself to breathe deeply, to take a grip on myself and to relax: all in vain. My eyes roamed over the first sentence, unseeing. Raising my head, I felt blood rush to my ears. I struggled through my text, goodness knows how, and then there followed questions about causes and solutions.

I lost my place once, causing a ten-second silence. After several hesitations, I simply repeated the words. Then came the first question: 'Do you think the present government's policy has been instrumental in causing exogenous disturbances?' I could not go to the toilet – that would have been really gutless. But what the hell are exogenous disturbances? My native wit came to the rescue. I replied, 'Would the questioner give a brief account of the concept of exogenous disturbances for the less enlightened students in the hall?' This was the tactic of an academic coward, but by this technique I struggled through my time allowance. And that morning killed stone-dead any ambitions I may have had of becoming a university lecturer.

I have to say that on such occasions I found my fellow students pretty intimidating. I saw them as the children of a privileged class, members of a virtuous circle, a good deal richer and more powerful and certainly more articulate than me, while most of those I had left behind me in Hunslet and Cumbria were on a downward spiral and would become relatively poorer. So, I had learned, the gap widens progressively, the poor getting poorer, and the rich relatively richer.

At the end of each weekday I would be jaded after a twelve-hour non-stop stint at the university. All the mature students were miles ahead of me, having been involved in some form of further education during their teenage years. My brilliant idea of leaving the rat race of manual labour and professional sport in pursuit of formal education had seemed stunning at the time but now I was having second thoughts.

However, I cannot deny that I found nearly all aspects of university life extremely stimulating. Among the bonuses were the discussions, the exchanges of ideas, the debates. All aspects of society existed within the campus: theatre, music, the media, politics, religion, sport; there was something for everyone. But still something nagged within me and it has never left me: my discomfort, my inadequacy on social grounds.

At the end of my first year, a series of exams had to be taken, success in which was essential if I was to go on to start my second and third years. To my horror, I failed statistics. What was I to do? Anne and I had made so many sacrifices. Now I needed the summer vacation to prepare and re-sit the exam. But we were desperately short of money, the overdraft was stretched to the limit, and more credit could not be obtained because of the national economic crisis. For this was the period of the 1966 sterling crisis, when the pound was taking a hammering and large sums were being poured in to stop its international value dropping through the floor. The government's solution was to cut back on public and private expenditure and, as the crisis continued through June and July, Prime Minister Harold Wilson imposed a severe credit squeeze.

My summer programme required credit because, as I needed the summer months for my assault on the September exam, my earning capacity was frozen. I could ill afford the cost in time and money of a return train journey to Cumbria but I had to see my bank manager. On the way I prepared a strategy, a proposition which would allow me to increase my borrowing at that difficult time. I suggested that he should send letters to those with overdrafts and request a reduction. And that he should lend my business the £200 I needed to live on from these repayments. The net result would be no increase in credit to private accounts. He agreed. Thus, because I had a business, I was able to resolve a personal crisis within a national crisis, and once more I was able to continue my studies.

To end the year on an even happier note, I won a Grade B for the re-sit of my statistics paper, largely through the private tuition I had been given by a friend of Roy Wilkinson, Tony Cox, now Professor of Sociology at Bristol. Tony sternly refused all payment for the hours of work he had put in on my behalf. He just wanted to know if Anne was a good cook. Learning that she was, he said the reward he would most enjoy would be a meal cooked by Anne at home. Of course Anne surpassed herself and we all enjoyed a wonderful evening.

Eventually my final year began and all I did, and dared to do, was study. In many ways, this was a shame. I had been doing some work for the Workers Education Association in co-ordination with Dr Chris Duke, a sociologist from Cambridge University, in the Chapeltown district of Leeds. Chapeltown is a black ghetto, and I had been asked to contribute to a course entitled 'Integration into British Society'. It was fascinating work, which led me to reconsider my own position. People who did not know me frequently assumed, because of my brown skin, that I was a foreigner, and I got used to being an outsider. But, face to face with the West Indians who lived in Chapeltown, I realised how very English I was. Theirs was a culture completely alien to mine: their life-style, language, clothes, food, relationships, sense of humour, music and dance, were all fascinating but had no relevance to my life. Yet, despite this, and despite their appalling lack of punctuality – classes had to be regularly delayed for half an hour or more because people were late, and then they would overrun – I was happy in their company. Everyone likes to be lionised, and I was treated with deference because of the way I had emerged as a brown person in a predominantly white society; I suggested the possibility that they or their children could do the same. I helped to start a savings scheme, attended their very animated Sunday services and, one year, chose their carnival queen. Putting this aside for study was a sacrifice, but one I knew I had to make.

It seemed as if some sort of metamorphosis was taking place within me. I was shedding my chrysalis and a new T. C. Thompson was emerging, slimmer but tougher psychologically. At the same time, though Anne and I shared a loving domestic life, a psychological barrier existed between us. It was as if fate would not allow us to enjoy our often ecstatic love until I had finally beaten down the demons that had haunted me for so many years.

Certainly there were times when it seemed that our love might soon be extinguished. I remained cruelly inflexible on insisting that my studies came before everything else when our love was crying out to be nurtured. I was certainly guilty of exploiting Anne's tolerance, her all too kindly nature, expecting her always to be subservient to me.

After all, these were the carefree 1960s, Cliff Richard and the Beatles, and Anne's emotional life had been drained dry during the seven years of my studies. But we came through and our love has remained, though possibly a bit battered, intensely dear to us.

I also made a discovery. During my long periods of revision as my course drew on, I found out that actually I had quite a good brain. But being twice the age of most of the students around me, my rate of understanding and recall was much slower. I could succeed but I must not allow the high flyers to deter my slower progress. After all, I told myself, I might well have been a high flyer myself had I enjoyed the right sort of nurture during my formative years. It was beginning to dawn on me that I really was getting an excellent return on my investment in education.

Another sacrifice was sleep. Fortunately I have never needed much. On one occasion during the final examination period I worked round the clock for thirty-six hours. I had to cut myself off from everything, including every aspect of normal life, if I was to pass the exam, and my days were spent in almost total seclusion.

However, this is the moment – before I try to describe the awful period of my finals – to tell of one thing which gave me lasting pleasure and pride during my time at Leeds. This was my involvement in Student Rugby League which had blossomed during my second year. It happened purely by chance. A nice man called Jack Abernethy (now Doctor Jack Abernethy) saw me a couple of times in the Brotherton, and said to himself, 'That looks like Cec Thompson whom I've seen playing for Workington Town, and used to see cleaning windows at Cockermouth Grammar School when I was in the sixth form.' Jack was with his best friend, Andrew Cudbertson, when he spotted me for the third time, and mentioned the resemblance to Andrew. 'What on earth,' said Jack to Andrew, 'would Cec Thompson be doing in a place like this, and dressed up in the way he is? I wonder if he's after the window-cleaning contract? If he is, his business has certainly expanded.' Andrew plucked up the courage to approach me and thus began the birth of Student Rugby League.

Andrew was a chemistry student from Hull, a Rugby League fanatic, with a bee in his bonnet. When freshmen arrive at university they are greeted by the secretaries of a multitude of societies: I think there were almost 200 of them when I went to Leeds, from ballroom dancing to Zen Buddhism, but – as Andrew noted with distress – there was no society or club devoted to Rugby League. When he learned that I was a genuine Rugby League international he was overjoyed and I found myself president and coach of the first official Student Rugby League club in the world.

A rugby-loving law student explained the constitutional niceties of starting a society: the biggest problem was that we had to be in existence for one year before the Students' Union would recognise us and give us a grant. In other words, we had to find the first year's cash ourselves. I at once took on the task of raising funds, and asked Eddie Waring to chair a quiz and film show at the university. Though we charged 7s. 6d. (37½p) a head we managed to fill the largest lecture-hall. Eddie refused payment. 'I'm only too pleased to help,' he told me in his famous growl. 'I just hope you and Andrew are successful in getting Student Rugby League off the ground. By the way, these students are the most attentive audience I've ever had before me!'

That was in 1966. We were solvent, thanks to Eddie, and even had enough money to buy two full strips, but what we lacked were opponents. We joined the Hunslet District League in the 1966–67 season, with a team that included players from all round the world: Chinese, Africans, Americans, Australians, New Zealanders and Canadians, as well as some who turned out for the University Rugby Union side on a Saturday and played Rugby League under a pseudonym on Sundays. It was a good season with eleven wins, two draws, and the award of the League's Sportsmanship trophy. It was all very enjoyable, but the biggest moment – the historic moment – was the first ever inter-varsity Rugby League match, when we played Liverpool at Widnes on 15 March 1968. It was as if a huge class barrier, between the educated classes and the world of Rugby League, had been broken down, and I had been in at the start. And that certainly wasn't going to be the end. As I reported in Leeds University's first *Rugby League Handbook* for the 1968–69 season:

During the bizarre days of October 1967 we waited for members to enrol: first ten came, then twenty, then forty members, and finally, by March of this year, over seventy students had joined. Our teams soon tasted victory. Something I have noticed is the difference between the disposition of the students towards the playing of Rugby League and that of regular clubs playing in the Hunslet League. The students approach it as a form of exercise, a release of inhibitions, while their opponents have a determined will to win since the game is often the focal point of their social lives.

There's more. This coming season, 1968–69, the club will have a pitch on the university grounds with excellent facilities, and an annual dinner, as well as a weekend in London with matches against two London college teams. And we mustn't overlook the tremendous debt we owe to Andrew Cudbertson, the founder of the club, who has been more than a secretary; at times he has carried the whole burden of the administration on his shoulders. If this season approaches the success and progress of the last it will be mainly thanks to his groundwork. And if we do achieve as much this coming year as in the year gone by I'll be more than delighted. I'm already thoroughly chuffed to have been chosen as club president for a second season.

Progress did indeed continue. Students throughout Britain discovered for themselves that Rugby League was a game that could be played for enjoyment as well as profit. I think until that time it was viewed by many as something like gladiatorial combat; you didn't so much mind watching others face the lions but you wouldn't want to do it yourself. Now all sorts of people joined in, from clergymen to miners, philosophers to financiers. Soon Manchester and Salford Universities were fielding sides, and then Sheffield and Bradford joined in, giving us a league of six; Lancaster, Hull and Nottingham expanded our choice of opponents still further. It was time to get organised on a national scale, and thus the Universities Rugby League Clubs Association was formed, quickly becoming the Universities and Colleges Amateur Rugby League Association (UCARLA) as polytechnics and colleges became involved as well.

Each season saw new developments and before long there were over fifty clubs taking part. In the early 1970s Sheffield became the first club to topple Leeds from its position of pre-eminence. Then in April 1973 an historic fixture took place when the first Student Rugby League international took place between British Universities and a World Student team. British Universities lost 11–17.

We now had the organisation to arrange such matches as Lancashire versus Yorkshire, the North versus the South, France versus Great Britain, and even – a tremendous tribute to Andrew Cudbertson's powers of persuasion – Oxford versus Cambridge. The importance of this last fixture can hardly be over-emphasised. For whatever reason, and however unjustly, Rugby League was still largely considered as just a game for aggressive up-and-under northerners. Thus League was not only denied access to a pool of talented potential players but also created a situation in which many students, even at northern universities, retained their ill-informed prejudice against the game. In other words, Rugby League was not only losing potential players, it was also alienating those who in future would become sports editors, television producers, advertising agency account holders and company directors. Student RL went a long way towards changing all that.

As time went on and the success of the game spread abroad it became obvious that the next logical step would be an international competition. The Student Rugby League World Cup was the original idea of a New Zealander, Bud Lisle, the president of the New Zealand Universities RL Council. He organised the inaugural competition in New Zealand in 1986 when the five countries taking part were Australia, France, Great Britain, New Zealand and Papua New Guinea. The tournament was a huge success and those five countries taking part agreed that the World Cup should become a regular feature of the Student Rugby League programme.

The next World Cup was held in England in 1989. Until then SRL had been organised and administered voluntarily. However, in November 1988, Malcolm Reid and Bev Risman, Gus's son, were appointed by the RFL to oversee the organisation as joint World Cup co-ordinators.

Many people worked hard to ensure that this first World Cup held in Britain was a success, and none worked harder than Bev. The main sponsors of the competition were the National Westminster Bank, the *Daily Telegraph* and U.K. Corrugated Ltd; Umbro provided the kit and Mitre the rugby balls. Eight countries took part: England, Scotland, Ireland, Wales, France, Holland, Australia and New Zealand.

To see such astonishing progress after our humble beginnings twenty-one years earlier made me extremely proud. The Scots wore kilts, the Dutch came in clogs: there was a truly international flavour to the opening events. Nor was the play a letdown; indeed, the standard of play in Student RL has to be seen to be believed; among those who have been associated with university clubs during their undergraduate days are the outstanding Great Britain international, Phil Clarke, and Barrie-Jon Mather, both of Wigan. The late Lord Derby, then president of the Rugby Football League, presented a magnificent trophy, sponsored by the National Westminster Bank, to the eventual winners, Australia.

Officials and players were accommodated at York University in July and August 1989. At the official reception I was proud to be able to greet the young men who had come from all over the world to play rugby, and proud too, I have to say, about my own contribution to Student Rugby League over the years. Of course most of the credit must go again to Andrew Cudbertson; without Andrew there would have been no Student RL at all but I cannot deny that without me it might never have got off the ground in the way it did.

In August 1992 ten countries took part in the third World Cup held in Australia: Australia herself, New Zealand, Papua New Guinea, Fiji,

Tonga, Western Samoa, England, Scotland, Ireland and Wales. And again Australia won.

Now already plans are afoot for the fourth World Cup, to be held in this country in August 1996 and to be sponsored by the Halifax Building Society. Definite starters are likely to be England, Scotland, Ireland, Wales and France, Australia and New Zealand, and ideally one or all of Papua New Guinea, Fiji, Western Samoa, Tonga and the Cook Islands. Morocco, with its large student population, should also take part, and Canada, the USA, Japan, Russia and South Africa may also be represented. In the event, I doubt that all the Pacific Islands will have sufficient funds to send teams but if only two are able to come, plus, say, Morocco, PNG and Russia, at least twelve countries would be represented to support the four home countries, France, Australia and New Zealand.

I am absolutely astonished by the roaring success which Student RL has become. Truly, out of a tiny acorn a mighty oak has flourished.

Chapter 9

In the weeks before my finals my legs had never felt so fragile. Surely no human being was meant to take such pressure. Judgement on the success or otherwise of my six years as a full-time student would be passed on my performance during the next two weeks. At the thought of it, my mouth felt as if it was stuffed with an old, sweaty sock. The examination hurdles along the way had taught me a lot about myself. I had derived a sort of masochistic pleasure from the long hours in which I was imprisoned in the library. At least, they were a good deal more comfortable and productive than the hours endured underground or on the assembly line by many of my old mates in Hunslet and Workington. If I were successful, a new future would open up for me. For my old mates, it would always be the next day and then the next day and then the day after that.

I feigned confidence as usual by garrulous behaviour: below the surface I was petrified. My hand would be shaking at the end of a three-hour exam, and there were to be nine such examinations in all. After about two and a half hours of any one of them my arm would ache like a stitch after intense physical exertion. I would mutter to myself, 'Cec, defy that pain, it's only in your mind. You can't let yourself down now, you've made too many sacrifices. You have learned to live with fear, now endure this next half hour.' Halfway through the exams I realised that my programme did not allow for any sort of break. I was afraid to stop; and began to prepare for the next exam almost immediately after the last was finished. As in my early days with Hunslet on the rugby field, I ran and ran and ran non-stop without any thought, without even trying to pace myself.

Sometimes my thoughts would stray to Anne and to memories of the early days of our relationship. I remembered how, after our first meeting, I had no idea how to approach her and bring her more into my presence. She seemed so controlled, so sure of herself. I was garrulous to a fault in my attempts to command her attention. We really had so little in common, and I was afraid of rejection. What would we talk about if I was alone with her?

Sometimes I used to shed real tears at the helplessness I felt in trying to comprehend the complexities of micro-economics and of other subjects I was supposed to be learning. And I worried desperately that no one had taught me how to cope psychologically with a series of long and difficult papers. I had not been coached as others had been at school. I kept reminding myself, 'You're not dumb, Cec. You were simply deprived.' Away from the examination hall, I slogged and slogged in our bedroom which had become my study. It was tough for Anne, for papers were everywhere; and the room was not to be tidied up, that was an order. She had an obsession with cleanliness and tidiness, but such personal priorities had to be waived. Nerves were at a premium and I tried hard to conceal my anxiety.

The last exam was the supreme challenge. A three-hour paper, not a question but a single word! Only an academic crank could think of such a crazy act. I will not disclose the professor's name who set this very remarkable paper. To my astonishment, as I looked at the sheet in front of me, the single word was 'Customs'. I had plenty of time to think about this single word and to start writing. I was unsure what was relevant or irrelevant to the exam, but eventually I started to write and some passages flowed from the heart. Obviously it would be too boring and of little interest to reproduce the whole of my paper but these passages give some of its flavour:

Customs can be handed down over many generations and can become a body of belief. So it is traditional to behave in a particular manner and according to custom. Hence the vast majority of the population can become victims, committed to an appalling, wretched life of beggarly misery. A good example is Galileo who published his discoveries of the universe and was put on trial by the Pope since they were seen to be contrary to the views of the church. The church was bound by custom (in this case by holy doctrine), rather than by reason. Galileo was put in prison while the advance of science in Italy was halted for many centuries . . .

Another radical who kicked against customs was Eleanor Marx, Karl's daughter. Her father wrote about plebeians, and Eleanor joined with them in her fight against injustice . . . and she was ridiculed by the establishment that tried to gag her. She was merely exposing the terrible exploitation of women . . .

The proletariat, as Marx called the working-classes, live very much according to sets of customs. Their lives are like living on a treadmill, with little change, an unvarying existence. The factory worker is hinged to the clocking-on system and regular hours of work. With mass production techniques the workers are involved in a variety of processes on giant conveyor belts which eventually deliver a finished product, such as a motorcar. It is a life of work, pub, club, package holidays, TV soaps, an orderly life dictated by customs. As technology advances, so do redundancies, because the customary way of life has been broken. Labour has become too specialised, and so occupational immobility arises. The working-classes have little freedom of choice such as the upper-classes enjoy with their many contacts or the middle-classes through their education. Most important, the working-classes, or the underclass, must work every day of every week to provide for their means of living. As their monthly mortgage has always to be paid they have no savings, or very little. They are tradesmen, semi-skilled or unskilled, at the lower or lowest end of the labour market . . .

Many of the labouring classes are unloved, struggle hard and long and never attain a foothold in the world. Their vast resources of energy and dogged hard work fail to break down the barriers to success which is held from them by customs. Herculean labours by a minority in the working-classes have gained political power for a more democratic society. They have pitted themselves against the system to produce a more credible world and have broken

down customs in which many had become disenfranchised. The
right to vote had been based on educational qualifications, property
rights and gender. Thus the vast majority were not represented
in Parliament . . .

Then the ordeal was over. Some had failed, the majority had passed.
It was almost a shock for me to emerge from that tormented period
to discover that I had actually gained an honours degree.

Even more shocking was that the *Yorkshire Post* had decided to
publish a full-page story on how an unknown factory labourer from
Leeds twice came to represent Great Britain at Rugby League, and
then earned for himself an honours degree. The national press picked
up the story and on graduation day, when the Duchess of Kent, the
Vice-Chancellor, presented me with my degree, a horde of reporters
and photographers bombarded me. I liked it, to begin with.

The next day, BBC television invaded our maisonette for three
hours for a fifteen-minute programme that evening; the day after that
I escaped the media to clean windows in Cumbria and earn some
money for a well deserved holiday, and a *Times* reporter interviewed
me up my ladder. Never underestimate the power of the press:
American friends saw this story in the *Washington Post* and sent me
the article, with the headline 'Window Cleaner to Honours Degree';
while Cec Mountford, president of the New Zealand Rugby League
and once a celebrated stand-off for Wigan, sent me a similar press
cutting from a New Zealand paper and congratulated me. Apparently
those six years of study had created a story of world-wide interest,
which bemused me as I got on with cleaning windows.

A spin-off from all this publicity was an invitation to become a
founder member of the BBC TV Advisory Council for 'Look North'.
Other members were the late Don Revie, manager of Leeds United,
probably the best football team in the world at the time; Jimmy Saville,
unknighted then and hosting 'Top of the Pops'; the Countess of

Harewood; Dorothy Hyman, the Olympic gold medallist; Patrick
Nuttgens, the chairman of the Advisory Council and principal of what
was then Leeds Polytechnic (now a university), who was well known
for his many programmes on television about architecture and city
planning; the York City treasurer; the editor of the Bradford *Telegraph
& Argus*; William Hill, who was headmaster of Myers Grove Comprehensive School, Sheffield, and a member of the public schools commission; and Baroness Alice Bacon. Important people, in other words,
and it was certainly flattering to be invited to join them. But meanwhile
what was I to do with my degree? I was invited to be a university
sports secretary, which was a most attractive offer, giving me a sabbatical
year involving travel to various countries, but my conscience would
not allow me to accept. I wanted to contribute to society; and I needed
to earn hard cash.

I turned over the alternatives. I was immensely proud of the way
my business had developed. My manageress, Shirley Hogan, has often
told people, 'Cec is generous to the point of being a fool, but he's no
fool or I'd not have worked for him these past twenty years.' Only
two people have ever been dismissed, one man for stealing and a
woman with alcohol problems. We have a very low staff turnover
because most of the employees are happy with us. If I feel that I have
hurt someone's feelings I'll make amends. Since many of my labour
force are female I usually send flowers. In other words, it is an intimate
and rewarding organisation, which has been part of my life now for
nearly forty years.

My business freed me to accept the coaching post at Barrow and
to raise myself above the numbing slog of manual labour. Later, when
I decided to become a full-time student, the business provided more
than just the £3 a week grant for my bedsitter: without the additional
income I could never have persuaded myself, much less anyone else,
that my dreams were viable. But for Jim's betrayal all would have been
straightforward, and as I survived even that, I suppose I should take
the advice of Kipling's 'If – if you can start again at your beginnings
and never breathe a word about your loss.

Choosing the right people to work for you is a major part of business success. When in 1963 I was rebuilding after the incident with Jim – I had no income, let alone a supplementary income, and had constant living costs – I took a tremendous risk in employing Dennis Williamson, a rugby player who could so easily have been injured. I held my breath every Saturday and prayed he would get through the match intact. He did, and he still works for me today, nearly thirty years later. Another association, which lasted the length of time, was with Brian and Katie, my brother- and sister-in-law. They allowed their home in the village of Flimby, near Workington, to be my registered office, forwarding my mail to wherever I was living, providing food and accommodation whenever I went to Cumbria, and in a hundred different ways helping to make my growing business a success.

If I am honest, however, I have to admit that my real breakthrough came in 1975 when I took on Shirley Hogan as manageress. Shirley had sold a highly successful hairdressing salon to spend more time with her young son and daughter and had reached the stage where she wanted to return to part-time employment. Though she was thrown in at the deep end when she came to work for me, and was a tyro in industrial cleaning, turnover soared as soon as she found her feet.

Some people do not suffer fools gladly. Shirley does not suffer fools at all. Yet she is always polite, as well as being completely trustworthy and thoroughly efficient. Efficiency is her watchword: 'I hate inefficiency', she has regularly been heard to say, and she means it. The company has grown dramatically since Shirley took over as manageress, especially when she introduced her own working methods; she has been worth her weight in gold.

That success has not always come easily, especially through periods of recession. Keen pricing against predatory competitors, combined with flexibility to the customers' needs, has been company strategy. But recessions can change the rules of the game in unpredictable ways. Several companies which have owed us large sums of money have been liquidated, which of course has put my company in jeopardy too. I have carried all the risks personally, and used my home as

collateral on loans to tide us through. But I am aware that I am not
the only one who depends on my success. We now have a labour
force of around 200, and their employment means nearly as much to
me as it does to them. Despite increasing size, and despite recession,
the company has remained a close-knit unit, which avoids bureaucracy
– I loathe bureaucracy – and our turnover has remained healthy. So
as long as we apply ourselves to the business enthusiastically and
energetically it will remain that way.

All in all, my cleaning business is something of which I am truly
proud. Logically, anybody who starts a business with no money (as I
did) cannot succeed, but sometimes you do, because you know that
if you don't succeed, you don't eat. But an equal share of the credit
must go to Shirley Hogan, a Cumbrian through and through, without
whose dedication and intelligent day-to-day control, we just might not
have succeeded.

Anyway, however successful my business, I really had no wish to
devote the rest of my life exclusively to industrial cleaning. So what
was I to do? In fact, there was really no question about it. I knew in
my heart that the only thing I really wanted to do was to teach. And
when the course tutor asked me why I wanted to teach, I replied that
I thought that, once I'd gained experience, I could be helpful to young
people. I would try to motivate them, stimulate their minds to learn
or at least give them some degree of self-assurance.

So I did a fourth year at Leeds University to gain a teaching diploma.
This brought me into contact with someone who was to become a
close friend and was to have an important impact on my life: Patrick
Maloney. Patrick was something of a 'silver-spooner', but with one
big difference: he was completely devoid of snobbery. He was also
desperate to play hooker for my university Rugby League team and,
since I was the sole selector, he used to follow me everywhere. To
start with I didn't know what to make of this grown-up schoolboy,

but soon I learned to appreciate him. Patrick had a student flat in Hunslet, near a famous pub called the Brass Moulders, built on the edge of what used to be an exceptionally tough area of Hunslet called Plevna (named after a battle in the Crimean War). The whole of the Plevna area was being pulled down for redevelopment, but the Brass Moulders had a long land lease and so still stood in this otherwise derelict area. Patrick adored Newcastle Brown ale. He was small and reminded me a bit of an Oxo cube with his short, quick legs, but ale allowed him to walk tall.

It was around this time that I encountered the Newsome Report (entitled *Half our Future*). I was studying for my diploma of education, and it seemed that the report, with its concern for the thousands of young people who leave school without tapping the surface of their potential, spoke directly to me. I was also invited to become a Trustee of the Cumbria Children's Fund and readily accepted.

Then early in 1969 I had to choose which type of school I wished to attend for teaching practice. I opted for a comprehensive where I hoped to meet some younger versions of myself, people I could inspire and influence. Patrick opted for a public school in order to rub shoulders with his own kith and kin. He went to Giggleswick, near Skipton, in West Yorkshire, and invited me to various social events at the school. Keen for any new and fruitful experiences, I went along and had my eyes opened to another world of which I had been quite oblivious.

I was incredulous that any section of society could lead such privileged lives, and this was emphasised by Giggleswick's gorgeous setting in the Yorkshire Dales. The familiar feeling came over me: how would I cope in such company, and in such a place? But, such is the value of education, this time I was able to hide my anxiety behind a veneer of fake confidence. It was my first acquaintance with the private sector of education, and the boys seemed, and almost certainly were, better mannered and behaved than those I was to meet in the school to which I had eventually been assigned, Calder High Comprehensive, Mytholmroyd, on the eastern edge of the Pennines, in West Yorkshire. But I was ready for my challenge.

My journey to Calder High involved leaving Morley at 7 a.m., and then two winter morning bus journeys through the industrial desolation of Halifax and the surrounding textile region, watching the sun rise over the mills. It was not inspiring. Still, it was what I had chosen.

One thing my experience had taught me was that the best way to beat fear is to scare it away by making a lot of noise. Some people who meet me think I'm naturally loud, when really I'm just naturally scared. Confronting a class for the first time was a case in point. I was flamboyant, certainly, but inside I was increasingly aware that my working-class background did not provide the sort of expertise and confidence that comes from a lifetime in academia. Many teachers go from school to university and back to school. To begin with, I thought this rather parochial and limiting, but I soon realised that to be a true professional this was the best sort of training to have. However, I never really managed that sort of absolute professionalism; but what I did achieve was a kind of empathy with my pupils.

Calder High catered for a predominantly working-class or lower-middle-class population. It was a clean, efficiently organised school of about 1,000 pupils, and a good place to learn something about teaching. My second subject was history, and the deputy headmaster, the late Ken Tomlinson, was an historian, so I got plenty of opportunity to watch him at work. As well as being a marvellous teacher, authoritarian but always fair, he was an excellent administrator and a gifted musician. I always used to go to evening concerts at Calder High and would see half a dozen members of the staff in the orchestra, playing wonderfully and of course without pay. Extra-curricular activities were always carried out without pay, yet they are what civilise a school.

Calder High also presented me with more opportunities to feel inadequate. Success in business or sport doesn't count for much when you're faced with thirty-five fifteen-year-olds who don't really want to be there, any more than passing a driving test means you're ready for the Lombard RAC rally. I was an honours graduate on the way to becoming a qualified teacher with a diploma in education, but with little competence and less confidence. All I had on my side was my old friend enthusiasm. Oh well, I thought, I'd not done so badly at rugby, despite my inadequacies: now for a repeat performance.

I may not have been a good teacher but at least I knew I could control a group of people. I had proved that as coach at Barrow, and the techniques of man management I had practised there seemed to work well enough in the classroom. Some teachers, and many members of the general public, think that good discipline in the classroom is synonymous with good teaching. That is not the case. Good discipline is important – you can't teach people who aren't listening – but real teaching is not about giving orders but about presenting knowledge in a way that students can understand and, at the same time, rouse their enthusiasm. And it is also about helping them, though this is very much more difficult, to understand that life is also a search for the fulfilment of ideals. For all this the teacher needs experience, and experience is exactly what I lacked. It was so long since I had been to school that I had forgotten the tricks. 'I hear you were a professional Rugby League player, sir?' said a voice from the back of the class. 'Who did you play for?' Naive in the pedagogical skills, I was naturally chuffed by this apparent interest in my life. I'm getting through to them at last, I thought, as I replied, and my lesson plan went out of the window. It was only later that I realised I had been conned.

My naivety threatened me in other ways. During the Easter period of 1969, I was applying for teaching posts for the school year ahead, and in those days when economics was a fledgling subject there were opportunities to start a new department from scratch. 'How great to be my own head of department,' I thought, believing my experience of life qualified me to take on such a responsibility, and assuming the job wouldn't really be so hard. Fortunately for me, and for my pupils, a few years intervened before I learned how wrong I was.

PART 4

TEACHING

Chapter 10

Perhaps it was because my CV was rather different from that of the usual applicant, or perhaps the interviewing panels were just curious to meet me but, whatever the reason, I managed to get shortlisted for most of the teaching posts for which I applied. I wanted to start my career in a comprehensive because I still fondly hoped to meet the person I was as a child and to give him – or her – the extra push that I had been denied. Dinnington High School is in the mining town of that name, in South Yorkshire, really quite a rural backwater, between Sheffield and Worksop. The school was, and is, a pure comprehensive with no predatory grammar school nearby to cream off the best. When they offered me a post I was happy to take it.

It was a wise decision. The staff there were superb – multi-talented, dedicated, competitive and ambitious – and the school catered for everyone from Oxbridge candidates to the barely literate. Facilities were first-rate: excellent drama and music departments, superb sports facilities, even a pit for car maintenance and, for pupils with learning problems, a youth club. It was comforting, amidst all this excellence, to learn that the deputy head, Les Tate, had played professional Rugby League with Leeds and Oldham, just as it was flattering to discover that another first-year teacher who started on the same day knew about me. She was from Workington and her father was a big League fan.

The school was absolutely chock-a-block with the underprivileged, the local community being engaged mainly in mining, agriculture, commerce and service trades. Out of school, away from the formal atmosphere of the classrooms, and especially on the sports field, I could develop a personal relationship with the pupils. I had been of their kind and so could afford to offer friendship. I could scrummage down with them, involve myself in rucks and mauls, in line-outs, allowing myself to be tackled, being careful how I tackled them. As far as the boys were concerned, this made it much easier to communicate in school. There was no class or colour consciousness in the school even though I saw no other blacks in the classrooms or even in the Dinnington area. Things were fine below the sixth form but with the latter I had to try to master my university notes and just gain experience with teaching at that level, my head of department taking most of the academic responsibility.

With the staff I continued my cocktail syndrome: talk, talk, talk, verbose with all and sundry, with anyone who cared to listen. My lack of confidence in any social relationship, the result of my upbringing, I suppose, continued. Sport, though, was a saving grace. I got involved with staff soccer, tennis and one game of Rugby Union. I damaged my weak knee scoring the winning try, and it swelled like a balloon the next day. That really was the end of my playing days. However, the PE department soon let the rest of the staff know that an international rugby player had joined the school, and of course the news spread quickly to the pupils. Never mind: it helped to give me some status where I might otherwise have been just a plain, middle-aged rookie teacher.

But, as always, there were problems. Here I was, partly responsible for pupils ranging from the potentially scholarly to the deprived by way of a largely indifferent middle section of the school. The gap between myself and the rest of the staff was immense, and increasing daily. I was ill at ease with my colleagues, who generally were much more composed, bookish, more up-to-date with current affairs. Their formal education had had plenty of time to mature between the ages of four and twenty-two, those eighteen years which I had tried to squash into seven. It was obvious that they were a good deal more professional than me. A self-taught person tends to become egotistical, and really pretty nauseating company, as he moves up the social scale. I was too tense among my new colleagues, the professional teaching class, and felt overwhelmed.

Every day I was in the middle of a hive of frenetic activity. So this is what teaching is all about, I thought. But, I told myself, 'You've simply got to live with this, Cec, for the rest of your life; don't get cynical or frustrated or let a chip grow on your shoulder.' Playing golf or tennis occasionally, I felt unkempt, aware of my dirty fingernails from manual work compared to my well polished, prosperous middle-class colleagues. But it was a good, though tough, apprenticeship.

My head of department, Malcolm Von Emloh, gave me a prolonged honeymoon period, allowing me time to get used to this new way of life. Though I was apprehensive, I also found this new world exciting but I seemed unable to behave like the rest of the staff. It seemed unnatural that when a bell rang at noon I had to eat. And my head of department, the deputy head, the headmaster, and all those bells simply had to be obeyed. I never tell people what they have to do; I always ask, and that is how I wish to be treated myself. But a rookie teacher is the lowest of the low, at the bottom of the hierarchy, and with every ring of the bell I was being reminded that at the age of forty-five I had just reached the lowest rung.

Authority always reminds me of a story I once read about the First World War when the British army had sustained 60,000 casualties on the first day of the battle of the Somme. Through the obedience to authority of two generals who had misunderstood orders from above but blindly followed what they had been ordered to do, innumerable families suffered immeasurable misery. John Morton, the headmaster, also imposed authority; of course it was essential in such a large school but, thank goodness, he was both an able and a charismatic teacher.

Never in my wildest dreams could I have imagined that I would one day work in a suit, a white shirt and a formal tie, and be paid a salary. It was a strange feeling. My colleagues on the teaching staff knew no other way of life. Many of them had parents who had lived likewise and they were simply following in their footsteps, never fully comprehending the psychology of the working-class, for many of whom they were now responsible. Those middle-class students I used to see walking round the university campus so nonchalantly with their files and briefcases, preparing to be teachers, remained a vivid memory.

Now I myself had to put on a cloak of sophistication. I could afford a measure of satisfaction but no complacency for I had been given a great deal more responsibility than I had enjoyed in my Barrow days. I am sure my colleagues were unaware of my psychological state: I was loud and bumptious, hiding a very thin edge of nervous tension to prevent a breakdown.

The group of teachers to whom I was attracted and eventually had joined were competent and successful members of staff. Now I had to be accepted by them. After a time I was invited to join them on their weekly visit to a pub in the next village called the Leeds Arms. This was enormously helpful to me. I gained a greater understanding of my new profession as well as a lot of information outside the formality of the classroom, and I made friends.

I was now pulling hard away from my original culture but found it difficult to come to terms with the complex problems of this uprooting. I was still gauche and somehow isolated in this new school world, lonely within a population of over 2,000 bodies. And I think it is worth noting that among that large body of pupils and 110 staff there was never another black face to be seen; and later, at Chesterfield, for only four of the seventeen years I was there, was there another non-white on the staff, a highly dignified and cultured Sikh, Amarik Marwaha.

Anyway, almost to our surprise, Anne and I rediscovered financial stability. September 1969 was an historic moment for us; it was the first time I received the salary that proved I was a professional person. At last we could start to pay off our debts and get out of the red. Nor was the bank the only institution I had to support: I could have filled a filing cabinet with the letters from lawyers, insurance companies, banks, tax inspectors (both VAT and PAYE) which I had received while I was a student. It seemed that now my problems were over: but then I had to learn to teach.

Good schools need good headmasters, and Dinnington amply reflected the calibre of theirs. John Morton was a Cambridge man, a no-nonsense disciplinarian who could be stern but was never unjust, a complete professional, whose influence was felt throughout the school. Outside the school he lost none of his virtues and added a couple of others: he had a delightful sense of humour and a sparkling personality. He was Dinnington's first head, and therefore the task of welding 2,000 pupils and a staff of 110 into a unit had fallen to him. He solved all the problems with aplomb, and I wonder if it is because of his influence that so many of those who taught under him went on to important positions in education, becoming advisers, inspectors, heads of departments and headmasters in their own right.

It is a fact that good teachers often have a range of other talents and enthusiasms. My own head of department, Malcolm Von Emloh, was one such. Not only was he a brilliant teacher who went on to become a headmaster, but he was also a terrific performer, demonstrating his musical and acting abilities in operetta. Similarly, Keith Millett, who joined the department after me, was not only superb in the classroom, but was justly rewarded by being made a deputy head. And he was also a Rugby League man, who played for Doncaster.

My salary may have been that of a professional at last but my approach, I have to confess, was still rather *ad hoc*, so I tried to disguise my lack of expertise behind a kind of extrovert bluster. It must have worked because most people just took me for an extrovert. Anyway, Dinnington High School was the start of my education as a teacher. I noticed that teaching is not just having knowledge: frequently expert outside speakers were invited to the school, and could not control a class despite all their knowledge. Yet discipline alone is not enough, for there is no point in getting students to listen if you have nothing to say.

One problem I encountered at Dinnington no longer exists, thank goodness. Before 1973, when the school leaving age was raised to sixteen, the low achievers had a year when, though the law compelled them to be at school, the system gave them nothing for which they could aim. From the ages of fourteen to fifteen, those pupils were simply there, in the way, and new teachers and probationers regularly had such classes dumped on them. They were difficult to handle. The girls would undo the top buttons of their blouses, trying to draw attention to their cleavages. The boys would compete for the most hilarious fart, producing ripples, violent blasts and squeaks amidst a miasma of noxious gases, which always struck me as odd behaviour in a mixed class.

While at Dinnington I was given a rugby team to manage. The head of PE, a stocky Welshman called Mike Pearce, approached me. 'So, you're the famous rugby player who has just joined the staff? You can get yourself down to the gym on Tuesday after school and meet your rugby squad for the season, an Under-15 team.' I was keen until I saw them: they reminded me of the film *The Dirty Dozen*, of that crew of criminals Burt Lancaster had to knock into shape before he could do anything with them. Appearances were not deceptive. They were as bad as they looked, a motley crew, all shapes and sizes, rotund, lanky, short, stroppy, and they looked at me as though they were a pack of rottweilers. I caught on quickly: I had been given the rogues of the fifth year, and they had no interest whatever in sport.

This can only get better, I thought, as I looked at them. It got worse. A group of three asked to speak to me in private. 'Go on then,' I said. Their reply was a chorus. 'Our parents have told us we should never speak to blacks!' 'That's fine,' I replied. 'We're going to get along very well.' Two more approached me. 'Here's a funny story, sir,' I was told. 'We went to the theatre with an English teacher. In the interval we asked, "Do you like Burns, sir?" He said, "Very much indeed!" So we stubbed a lighted cigarette on the back of his hand!'

It might have been easier had we been playing Rugby League. But Dinnington plays Union. Part of the teacher's responsibility is to referee the home matches. I had never realised how difficult the game of Rugby Union is to referee, nor had I studied the differences between the two codes. Despite all my experience with Barrow and my coaching course at Lilleshall I was still out of my depth, baffled by those Union rules. League was engraved on my system, and those line-outs, mauls and rucks seemed extraordinarily complicated. I had to rely on the boys to guide me, but I also had to be circumspect. If you do not control young people they soon spot your inabilities and come to control you. It was a case of keeping my head when all about me were losing theirs, and then adding a mixture of enthusiasm and humour to the Kipling while they put the blame on me! School sport depends on the voluntary activities of a select band of devoted teachers who, with no financial reward and at great expense in terms of their time and energy, nonetheless forge the sportsmen and women of the future. Their dedication is tremendous. It is also infectious, and soon I was working as hard as any of them. It may be unpaid, but the most rewarding aspects of teaching, for teacher and pupil alike, often are. I had also crossed the frontier from League to Union, and I was enjoying it.

One particular incident will always remain with me. I was refereeing one of my home matches at Dinnington and awarded a controversial try; as we waited for the conversion I heard the opposition under the posts complaining about the decision. 'He should never be refereeing,' said a voice. 'He knows nowt abaht game, he's a bluddy Paki!'

Maybe this was partly true but, by the end of the season, and using mostly third-degree tactics, I had made my reprobates into a useful team, and we even won a cup at a rugby tournament in Sheffield.

Also I won through rugby at Dinnington some unlikely friends. The deputy head asked me if I would take a particularly obstreperous youth under my wing and put him into my rugby squad. This lad was 6 feet tall and weighed about 13 stone, with 'I love you' – improbably – tattooed on the back of his fingers and a butterfly between each index finger and thumb. His smoking fingers were browner than my skin. His father was in jail for incest, and of the ten kids in his family four were deformed, bow-legged or deaf. During his first training session I told him he must keep his eye on the ball when receiving it. I played opposite him and we both jumped for a high-kicked ball. I landed a split second before him, almost on his foot. 'You've broken my bluddy foot, sir!' he yelled. A little while later he was watching the ball when about to receive a pass and I tackled him, my shoulder sinking into his guts or a trifle lower. He screamed, 'You've crushed my balls, sir, you've really crushed my balls!' I apologised and told him he was in the team on Saturday.

This uncontrollable boy was frightened to death, and only played one game, yet I must have got through to him somehow. I invited him home for meals, and once, when Anne was ill, he sent me a box of Roses chocolates and a bottle of Lucozade, though he asked me not to tell anyone of his kindness. Again, one Christmas he brought us a chicken. Later I discovered that he worked in a factory which prepared chickens for supermarkets where he earned the money for his fags, booze and girls, but by then the chicken, the evidence, had been consumed; even so, I did not dare to tell Anne this story. Eventually I persuaded him to join the Royal Navy, and wagered him that he would not last the initial month when they sorted out the soppy candidates. Each week he telephoned me from Portsmouth to say, 'I'm still here, sir!' The navy removed his tattoos and we have remained friends.

In all, I was at Dinnington High School for five years, and when I left I was far wiser and more confident than when I began. Two memories remain from that time, one to make me smile, the other to haunt me for life. On the first occasion a younger member of the school, to whom I was talking about work, said, 'My dad doesn't like blacks and says I must not talk to them – but I like you, sir.' The other comes not from the school but from a school trip. We used to take a group down to London to see the sights. It was an educational visit, taking in the Bank of England, Westminster Abbey and so on, but it left us a bit of time on our own so Keith Millett and I took a group of the older pupils for a quick drink in the Swiss Cottage area. A military type strolled into the bar, moustache bristling and umbrella carried at the slope, and looked at me. 'I didn't know they were letting niggers in here!' he announced.

I was devastated. All I had built up, my middle-class life, the respect of my pupils, the friendship of my colleagues, seemed to have been swept away by this bigot's remark. I felt as if I had been exposed as a fraud, which was ridiculous. I had earned all I had achieved; it was the military-looking man who was the fraud because, despite the plummy accent and expensive clothes that disguised him as a gentleman, no gentleman would speak like that. But it took me a long time to learn to see it that way. We drank up and left the pub in silence; none of my companions ever mentioned the incident again.

A different sadness was the death of Michael Mollan, the director of studies at Huddersfield, who had been such an inspiration during my three years there, and the man to whom more than any other I owed my place at university. Anne and I had been invited to his home several times since I had left the college. They were always delightful evenings and we got to know the family very well. His wife, Annette, told us that Michael had taken a particular, almost paternal, interest in my career, and that my achievement in winning a university place had been a source of great personal delight to him. I was honoured when Annette asked me to be a bearer at his funeral, though it was a sad, solemn duty. There are only a few friends to whom you can reach out for help when life becomes especially difficult, and Michael was one of them.

It was during my time at Dinnington that our son Mark was born. Anne and I had always wanted a child but to give that child a good life meant putting parenthood off until I had completed my course of formal education. And of course our financial problems had also to be resolved. Then there was a third consideration: I was concerned about our child's skin colour. I did not want to inflict on another the confusion I had been through, nor cause problems for Anne. I could not imagine what it would be like to be a white woman with a black child, but I could guess. It was only after I had acquired professional status that I had the confidence to become a father.

At the time Anne and I were living in the tiny village of Woodsetts, about five miles from Dinnington. It had a population of little more than 400, and was dominated by the early Victorian church of St Mary.

It was a tranquil village and our house not only had two living-rooms and three bedrooms but a hundred yards of garden with rose beds, a small orchard, a pergola, a vegetable garden and a greenhouse! After a while we had a kitchen, designed by Anne to the last detail, built on to the house. It was idyllic.

My appointment to Dinnington involved the patient Anne, for several months during the winter of 1969–70, in making a round trip of eighty miles every day back to her job in the West Riding before she managed to get a transfer to a similar post in the Rother Valley in South Yorkshire. Then Mark was born in Jessop's Hospital, Sheffield, on 26 August, 1973 and was baptised in St Mary's Church on a windy yet sunny day in October.

Education, it seemed to me, was the key to everything, and I was so committed to education that we enrolled Mark, at three years old, in a local kindergarten. At home, too, the pressure on the boy continued, and I was forever busy with Ladybird books, keen for him to read as soon as possible. By four, he was in the local junior school, and at five, I introduced him to *Speak and Spell* and *Speaking Maths*. Just before his sixth birthday, he began piano lessons with the organist at Chesterfield's 'crooked spire'. I had left Dinnington by then – so that he took a grade a year in piano exams, reaching grade 5 at the age of eleven. At the age of six, he was also put into a county chess competition and lost in the Under-9s' semi-final, an achievement photographed and acclaimed in the local press. Then he was given a computer! But all that was in the future. In the summer of 1974 my main concern was a new job I had accepted and the need for us to sell our lovely house and to buy another in Chesterfield.

Chapter 11

Most teachers need to change schools if they are to win promotion, and I was no exception. I applied for a number of jobs and among them wrote to Chesterfield Grammar School for the dual posts of head of economics and master-in-charge of rugby. I thought I had no chance but much to my surprise I was called for interview.

Anne and I were now parents with only one income coming in, so to cut costs we decided to sell Anne's car. We took a would-be buyer out for a spin, and he was being taught how to change gear in a country lane when a drunken driver ploughed into the rear of the car. I was in the back seat, suffered fractured ribs, and found myself spitting blood. After four days in hospital the day came for my interview at the school. I asked the headmaster if he could possibly delay the appointment since I thought I could get out for an interview the following day, and fortunately he agreed. It was now a question of persuading the doctor to let me out. I disguised the pain I was suffering and intensified my desperation for the post; and he agreed. Anne took me to Chesterfield as I could not drive, and when I got there I could only speak in a low voice – possibly giving the impression that I was rather an introverted character – but to my complete and genuine astonishment I was appointed and against Oxbridge opposition too, which was good for my ego, if not for my soul.

It was an impressive appointment. Dinnington High School had been a tough but useful initiation into teaching; Chesterfield Grammar School was a kindergarten by comparison, an academic, traditional all-boys school founded in 1589. Many of the staff had been at the school for over twenty years, and about a quarter of them were old boys. A small staff turnover is always a good recommendation for a school.

I began at Chesterfield in the autumn of 1974 with one probationary assistant. The department then consisted of twenty-four upper-sixth and nineteen lower-sixth pupils; when I left in 1991 it had grown to ninety-six sixth-formers, 135 GCSE and 127 social studies pupils, a total of 358, with a staff of three full-time and two part-time teachers under me. Moreover, my department's results were outstanding, a source of great pride to me. Alongside the syllabus, we also taped television documentaries of current affairs and followed them with in-depth discussions. At the same time the upper sixth wrote weekly essays in proper examination conditions from Easter through to the examination period in June. By a combination of hard work, a relaxed manner and a sense of humour, we ploughed through this tough programme with total success. They were hectic days, but we proved ourselves a hugely successful department.

Success breeds success. Parents wanted their sons to join a department which regularly achieved good results; and the students, after their initiation into my department via social studies, wanted to stay on. So my department became over-subscribed and I was given more staff. Over the years an average of 91 per cent gained A to C grades at GCSE level, and at 'A' level 50 per cent got A or B grades and 96 per cent a pass; indeed a 100 per cent pass-rate was not unusual from time to time. My department's success was proven. On the rugby field, too, we were successful. At times a key player in my 1st XV would want to leave school at sixteen and I would encourage him to stay on. I did not want the team to be weakened and I felt able to guarantee that he would get his 'A' level in economics, even if I had to give him private tuition at home. Often my teaching programme involved visits to hospital wards or to students at home. I would take them homework and reading material and my classrooms really became quite extensive! Any cock and bull story about being late for school or missing homework would always result in a telephone call to the boy's parents. My reputation soon got around but, more important, I would not allow misfortune to prevent students from achieving their potential.

At the same time I was going from strength to strength as a teacher, developing more and more self-belief. My history and track record at Chesterfield made me realise that I was really quite good at teaching – which I had certainly never believed before. Boys who were disruptive in other classes were automatically placed in mine. This had happened at Dinnington too and was a great boost for my ego. Here I was, a former scrubber in a forge, a driver's mate, performing what conventional teachers were apparently unable to do, control unruly students.

I had arrived at Chesterfield when the school was already on the verge of change. I am not a political animal but even I was aware of the tension between the local authority and the school over the school's future. The council wanted the school to become a comprehensive, part of the national system; the school, its parents and its governors, wanted it to remain a grammar school. In the end there was a compromise, called the 'Doncaster plan' (though never used in Doncaster nor, I suspect, anywhere else), by which Chesterfield School lost its first and second year, but parents could choose to send their boys there from the third year through to the sixth if they wanted to.

When I joined the school I wanted most of all to meet my predecessor. He had been an excellent teacher, who also took responsibility for the school's stage productions. He was a devout Christian – and, more important, a good and kind man – who had been at the school for more than twenty-six years. His was a hard act to follow: not only was he highly respected as an individual, but equally telling was his academic performance with first-rate results maintained year after year. 'Spike' Jones, as the boys called him, was suffering from terminal cancer, and his wife really did not want me to see him. However, there must have been a discussion at their house because later she phoned me back: 'Yes, my husband *would* like to see you'. We discovered that we had affinities because apart from being economics teachers we both had a passionate love of the Lake District. We also had dissimilarities: he had been a major in the army, while I had been a stoker in the navy. His rank was not a complete surprise to me. Many of the staff had held high positions in the services because grammar school teachers were graduates and graduates before the Second World War were

automatically middle-class. When the regular army officers got themselves killed or promoted these new officers filled the gaps, and several
of them climbed rapidly through the ranks. This had two effects when
they returned to teaching. It meant that they were capable and decisive,
and it meant that they were used to being obeyed. At Harrow the
boys doff their boaters to the beaks; at Chesterfield Grammar School
the boys doffed their caps to the staff. It was all rather daunting.

At my first meeting with my predecessor, little was said about
teaching, and nothing about economics. Instead we metaphorically
roamed the Fells, until I recognised the fatigue in his face and took
my leave. A few days later, his wife telephoned to say that my visit
had been like a tonic to her husband and that he seemed to have
recovered a little of his usual cheerful self. She asked if I could come
for another chat, whenever it was convenient, and I felt privileged to
be invited. Our second meeting was as enjoyable as our first as we
exchanged memories of the Lakes. But within a few weeks he had
died. He had been a brave man in war, and a braver man in peace.
Before my arrival he had continued to teach for twelve months, despite
the pain, just to keep the department going.

I once went to Nottingham Playhouse to see a play called *Gentleman
Jim*. It was about a public toilet attendant who dreamed and every
dream was a sketch in the play. Thus, in one he wanted to be a fighter
pilot; in another, a cowboy, and so on. The obstacles between his
dreams and reality were often the 'O' and 'A' levels required for
university entry. This production reminded me of my dream when
cleaning windows in schools, seeing the teachers at work, and fantasising
that I might one day work alongside them. My dreams had become
reality, but I also knew that many people are promoted to roles in
which they do not shine; indeed, in which they are often scarcely
competent. In a sense it had already happened to me several times. At
each stage of my career, at first I had only just been able to cope and

then eventually mastered the knack. At each stage – when I first signed for professional Rugby League, wrote my first article, made my first appearance on television, went to Huddersfield and to university, started and then restarted my business, or began my teaching career at Dinnington – I had worried that I might have taken on too much. And so, though later I had become the head of a department in a first-rate grammar school, I wasn't going to get complacent about my teaching skills.

There are many lessons to learn from life, and most of them are best learned early. I was a late developer but this much I do know: that I am a survivor, and that I can cope in most surroundings. Of course, to cope is not always easy. I have often done without sleep in order to follow up some idea or concept, and have frequently had to hide my ignorance behind a noisy, good-humoured façade.

Another lesson I have learned is that, when I meet new people, who are not aware of my background, they happily accept me as one of them but, whenever I stepped back into my old environment, all too often I was again the professional Rugby League player or the window-cleaner in their eyes. This was not particularly strange because in Chesterfield, as the head of a department, I was emphatically 'Sir'; and this made me realise just how complex the business of class really is. My speech had changed along the way, not deliberately but through a kind of evolution: I had hardly noticed the change until Border TV made their documentary, and my old rugby captain asked me when I had acquired the plum in my mouth. This has undoubtedly opened doors. Slowly, over the years, my voice lost its regional identity and, however it came about, a 'posher' accent was certainly a help when I began to teach at Chesterfield.

During my first terms I certainly needed all the help I could get. The number two in the department, a competent economist, was grieved to learn that he had been overlooked for promotion to head of department and so left to join another school. Another member of staff, who had been in charge of rugby, felt hurt that a newcomer had relieved him of his authority and responsibility. Both men had friends who would be happy to see me fail. The pressure had been intensified when, at the staff dinner-dance before I arrived, the headmaster announced that an international sportsman had been appointed. Such an announcement can prove an awful mistake since great things would be expected. Equally galling was that people would compare my results with those of my predecessor. Yet I refused to be intimidated. As head of the department I felt the burden of responsibility and intended to put all I had into the job.

The boys, I am sure, must have been taken aback by my approach to teaching. My predecessor had been quietly spoken, quietly authoritative in his ex-army way, and suddenly here was this weird flamboyant dictator. I was confident I could get good results from the boys, but until I did I felt I had no credibility in the school. My assistant, Malcolm Bride, was a probation teacher in his first year out of college. He was baby-faced, quiet and reserved, but nonetheless extremely competent. During the summer after the examinations I think I was as worried as the candidates, because I realised that my department's status, and indeed my own status as head, would be based on my results. When they came through they were the best in the school, both in the percentage pass rate and in the quality of the grades. Of the twenty-four boys in the upper sixth, fourteen received grade 'A' and only one failed.

However, I still had to tread warily. The head of PE was a soccer fanatic with a corresponding dislike of rugby, and it wasn't always easy to get the assistance I needed. But slowly and surely we made progress: Chesterfield School was in the County Cup final three times, won the Under-18s' Cup once, were three times County finalists for those above 18, were Under-15 County Champions once, Under-17 County Champions twice, and we also won the County Sevens tournament on one occasion. I became a county selector and served for five years as county treasurer. County selection was interesting. Often the selectors wanted to promote players from their own school into the county team. I had the impression that selectors would trade with each other, supporting each other's votes. In Derbyshire, two schools dominated the county team and, there was no doubt about it, they were outstanding schools. But it is undeniable that, once my exuberance had won me a place on the selectors' panel, other schools – including, I have to say, mine – won a greater representation. Nor do I think there was any favouritism involved. Chesterfield School was becoming highly respected throughout the county for the standard of its rugby.

Thus, as time went on, and my rugby results became as pleasing as my academic results, I found both activities gained in popularity. I had to insist on two more teachers to help with the rugby, and we were overworked in the economics department. One indication of how well established rugby had become, and an indication also of the calibre of the 1st XV, is that it became almost a tradition in the school for the 1st XV captain to become school captain. Most of the players became prefects, and every year most won university places, including several who went to Oxbridge.

To improve my Rugby Union coaching skills, I applied to go on a coaching course for the Union game, organised by the RFU coaching staff at Bisham Abbey. The aim of the course was to help improve the game at Under-18 level throughout England. Nearly 400 applied for thirty places; because I was a Derbyshire selector and helped with the county coaching, and definitely not because I had once been a professional rugby player, I was accepted. In fact, I had learned to avoid any mention of Rugby League when in the company of these Union buffs. I said I had been president of Leeds University rugby, and omitted the word 'League'. It was shameless deception, but it worked.

I found myself among the cream of the Under-18 coaches from around the country. The services were well represented but the majority were from public schools and grammar schools. In other words, the middle classes dominated. Though I had acquired a degree of social panache – enough anyway to overcome any difficulties my colour might cause – I was still aware of my Rugby League background. The course went well. In fact, after two years as a professional coach at Barrow, and two more years coaching at Leeds University, I found it reasonably easy to coach at schoolboy level. On the penultimate day of the course, each coach had to handle the whole squad for ten minutes in front of the current England coach, and on the last day there was a written exam. I felt pretty confident about the whole of the course; in fact, it seemed to me that I had left most of the others standing. Then on the last day I was asked if I had played Rugby League.

I was taken aback to have such a direct question put to me on the last day of the course when I thought I was home and dry. I like to think that I had impressed them so much that they had checked on my background but I certainly wasn't sure how they would react to my career in League. Startled, I answered immediately, without think-ing, that I was an economist and, as a sideline, I was interested in rugby. Actually at that time I didn't know of any black player who played Rugby Union, and only three or four who played Rugby League, which must have made it pretty easy for them to identify me. Though we were a happy and integrated squad, working hard mornings and afternoons, and enjoying a few beers in the evenings, and though my performance on the field had equalled anything the others had managed, I was the only one who was not awarded a coaching certificate. I detected a whiff of apartheid about this decision that had nothing to do with race but everything to with the rugby codes.

I find it bad enough, and sad enough, that some people should dislike me because of the colour of my skin. How much worse and how much more ridiculous that I should be cold-shouldered because I had played the 'wrong' sort of rugby. The apartheid system which Rugby Union imposes on professionals, past as well as present, should be extinct in a society that calls itself democratic. Even the present 3-year stand-down period is appalling. I find it daft that though much legislation is being passed these days regarding race and sex equality, so simple a matter as this is allowed to survive.

Those who have moved from the amateur to the professional code have caused many problems over the years. I suppose that two of the most illustrious names in recent times are those of Jonathan Davies and Martin Offiah but there are many others. An equally prominent example in an earlier decade was David Watkins, who in 1967 exchanged his Wales fly-half shirt for a wage from Salford RLFC. David was a hugely gifted player whose wonderful career included captaining Wales and the British Lions. He was born with no silver spoon in his mouth: he was a shift worker on the shop floor at British Steel. But this became more and more incompatible with his Rugby Union commitments, so his career was rearranged. He ended up as a rep, with a company car, though he had no licence, and was given five months' paid leave prior to the British Lions tour of New Zealand in 1966. I am not suggesting that David did not become a hugely competent rep and an asset to his company, but I am suggesting that the advantages of playing Rugby Union can be worth just as much as the money League players get paid. Nor do I complain about these things happening. I just complain about the way Union's sham-amateurs adopt a pose of superiority. At least I always acknowledged my debt to Rugby League and did not hide behind some hypocritical notion of amateurism.

When I was on tour in France with the 1st XV from Chesterfield School in 1984, I was chatting one evening with my headmaster and my assistant coach to a New Zealander who had been brought over by a French Rugby Union club. He told us that he had been provided with employment, a car, and a lump sum of money. At that time I found this quite astonishing for the so-called amateur code, but of course the hypocrisy is essentially British. Other countries interpret the rules surrounding the amateur status of Rugby Union in a rather more sensible way. Recognising that payment is bound to happen, they allow it to be open instead of hiding it behind a semblance of gentlemanly conduct.

I have referred constantly to the British class system: the gulf between the two codes originates in and reflects class division. It is also regional, an indicator of the north-south divide. The major public schools, except the Catholic ones, are in the south, while the manual workers who provide the fodder for Rugby League come from northern industrial towns. The situation is changing but it hasn't changed enough yet. Any contemporary Richard Hoggart wanting to analyze the classes and

regions of Britain could do worse than begin with an examination of
the rugby situation in Britain today; any academic with a wider brief,
hoping to show what differentiates outmoded Britain from the rest of
the modern world, should start by looking at the curious way this
country treats its rugby players.

Will Carling, England's Rugby Union captain, has said in a broadcast
that he is quite willing to accept sponsorship money but not payment
for playing because, at the age of sixty, he would like to think that
he had enjoyed an *honourable* (my italics) as well as a successful career.
What on earth does he mean by that? Carling is a fine fellow, an
exceptional player and an influential captain. But a little reflection
about his background suggests, first, that he could afford to think like
that – public school education at Sedbergh, army scholarship to Durham
University and, second, that he is being rather disingenuous. He may
not have received cash payments for playing, as I did, but can he really
pretend to have got anything less out of the game in material terms?
He owes everything he has achieved in his life to rugby, every bit as
much as I do. The rewards of Rugby Union are indirect but just as
tangible as the rewards of Rugby League.

In fact, Carling and Brian Moore, the England hooker, have led the
way in demands for off-the-field earnings which are now permitted
by the International Rugby Board. It was said that all members of the
England and Scotland teams who played in the 1994 Calcutta Cup
were on £2,000 a man for the time and effort spent on off-the-field
promotion on behalf of sponsors. Carling himself is said to earn
something like £100,000 a year from off-the-field activities related to
the game. And Brian Moore has said, 'I wouldn't mind being a
semi-professional player and those players who eke out a meagre living
should certainly have their talent rewarded properly.'

These old controversies had been boiling away at Twickenham and
at other fortresses of the Union game in Britain for four or five years,
when in February 1994 the New Zealand RFU boldly declared itself
in favour of the game becoming professional. Of course, before this
could actually happen, there would have to be a two-thirds majority

vote in favour of the change by the International Rugby Board (IRB). And though New Zealand could count on support from Australia and maybe South Africa, they would be opposed by the British delegates (though almost certainly not by the players). Eddie Tonks, the then chairman of the IRB and also chairman of the New Zealand RFU, said, 'We have got to try to change the IRB regulations,' and admitted that sham-amateurism was rampant. 'We are so close to professionalism at the moment. We either have rules we can all comply with or you cut the rules out.'

About a year after Eddie Tonks had spoken, Phil Harry, Australia's leading Rugby Union official, predicted that amateurism in Union would be a thing of the past by the end of 1995. He asserted that his country's top RU players would be able to reap increased financial benefits: the players 'will get a lot more than they do now,' he said.

This pronouncement was followed by the startling news that Australia and New Zealand had already decided to organise a wholly professional Rugby Union tournament during the three months of March, April and May in 1996. Moreover, the IRB had already agreed to hold a special meeting in Paris at the beginning of August 1995 to debate the issue of professionalism after hearing the recommendations of last year's IRB chairman, Dr Vernon Pugh of Wales.

Apparently Australia and New Zealand propose to organise a tournament for eight teams, two from NSW, Queensland and ACT, four from New Zealand's North Island and two from New Zealand's South Island. Each squad will contain thirty players and the tournament itself (which will take the place of the present Super-10 competition) is said to be worth £30 million. It was thought that the players taking part would be paid at least £25,000 a year and the matches will be televised live on the Sky Network pay TV station in New Zealand (in which Murdoch does not have a share) and on Channel 7 in Australia (in which Murdoch does have a share). The Australian Rugby Union say they have £10 million available as 'seed money' to fund the competition, and it is widely believed that as many as twelve Wallabies and nineteen All Blacks will be playing and that each could earn £80,000 a year from their normal jobs and their rugby payments.

Needless to say, Twickenham has been appalled by all these developments and declared that this was no way to protect Australian and New Zealand players from the depredations of Rugby League down under. While Twickenham was sounding these dire warnings, Dudley Wood, the RFU secretary, was under fire from the chairman of the National Heritage Committee, who declared that until the RFU amended those of their regulations which discriminated against Rugby League no further funding from the Sports Council or any other body which distributed public funds should go to the RFU or any of its member clubs.

The National Heritage Committee also recommended that no further distribution of National Lottery proceeds should be made to Union clubs until Rugby League was treated equally with all other sports in Union regulations. In addition, the committee established conclusively for the Inland Revenue that the benefits Union players now receive – housing and cars, for example – certainly represent income and are accordingly taxable. The committee also noted that the IRB had conceded that the word 'amateurism' in the context of Rugby Union was in many cases no more than a veil.

Of course all this was already well known to anyone who had been involved in League/Union conflicts over the years but it was good to have it all aired and be led to believe that just possibly the end of hypocrisy was in sight. Incidentally, the argument put forward to the RFU that a stand-down period (for a League player wishing to return to Union, presently three years) was an essential defence against the depredations of League brought the interesting retort from Chapeltown Road that over the years Rugby League had drawn only 8.1 per cent of its players from Rugby Union.

My own belief is that Rugby Union, at any rate in Britain, simply cannot afford to become professional at club level though I am equally sure that international players will be paid for playing, presumably as soon as 1996. Of course, whether Rugby Union officials will ever learn to tolerate the game of Rugby League, as a game, is another matter altogether. Anyway, in 1986, after twelve years of coaching schoolboys, I decided that I would have to bring my involvement with Chesterfield School's rugby to an end. I was still the managing director of a cleaning company with a labour force of around 200 and my teaching responsibilities were increasing by the term.

When I stood down there were over eighty boys and three members of staff taking part in Rugby Union. There was also a strong link with the local club, and many of our lads played for Chesterfield RFC. Indeed, we were on the verge of leaving for a tour of various rugby-playing American schools (free accommodation, only transport to be paid for) when one of my staff in the economics department was promoted to be head of department at another school and I simply had to put my academic responsibilities first. It seemed a strong legacy to hand on, and my successor as master-in-charge of rugby was a committed member of the Chesterfield club. But, within twelve months, rugby ceased to be played at our school. In local politics the right wing demands that everything has a price; the left gives power to the unions. Between the two of them they ensured that teachers must work to a contract, and that contract excluded the many long unpaid hours needed to get a rugby team motivated. This had to be a loss for everyone in the school, students as well as staff.

At Chesterfield, and I know at many other former grammar schools, the sports field allowed a welcome break from the strict classroom atmosphere: we were on Christian name terms, and the emphasis was on self-discipline, courage, fair play and honest endeavour, rather than obedience. Often the games were just good, straightforward fun, as when – at the end of a term or season – I might find myself rolled in the mud. Strictness was sometimes needed, because obviously a team must play together as a team, but it was strictness tempered with respect for what each boy could contribute. Now all that came to an end, thanks to the conflicts of local politics, the same conflicts that were eventually to close Chesterfield Grammar school itself in 1991.

My weekly routine at Chesterfield was packed tight. On Saturday mornings I used to referee the school rugby matches. On Tuesday and Thursday evenings, after school, I coached the various school teams, taking the 1st XV on Wednesday afternoons. On Sunday mornings I coached the county team. I had to use Sunday afternoons and evenings to catch up with my marking – and I still had my cleaning business in Cumbria to attend to. On September evenings at the beginning of a new school year, when the classroom teaching was over, I was out on the sports field, coaching youngsters, many for the first time. By October some of these novices might even be playing for the school and moving on to the county trials. We would practise mauls, rucks, line-outs and scrummages until the setting of the late summer sun. It was sheer joy, and I look back at the team photographs of those years with real affection. And I know the affection was returned for the reunion dinners were and still remain gloriously happy occasions.

At one of those dinners I was invited to speak. Before my speech began, the master of ceremonies rang a ship's bell to toast those in their eighties, then seventies, sixties, and so on every ten minutes. There was a toast for the fathers and sons present, and finally for the grandfathers, sons and grandsons. The evening ended in the early hours with each school house going to a designated area of the room for the school song, which was then sung with a chorus from each house.

I was made an honorary old boy and presented with a tie after my talk. As usual, I was the only black person in the room. In the company of all those eminent people, the doctors and judges and professors and knights of the realm, I considered the strange route my life had taken. To be accepted as one of them, to be part of all this, was deeply moving. When I got home that night I reflected on how life keeps unfolding, offering new wonders and new experiences to those who open their arms to it.

However, the happiness I derived from such occasions was nothing compared to the examination successes that kept piling up. It was obvious that with some students there was little parent involvement. In those cases I tried to encourage the boys to want to learn, to think and to understand. After a few months, these youngsters, of average and below-average ability in many cases, showed a huge improvement in their performance. Some, by the time they entered the sixth form, an event which had often lain beyond their wildest hopes, would be thriving academically. Similarly, on the sports field, when some boys entered the school they had never played rugby before or had shown no talent in their previous school. Then suddenly some latent skills emerged, and the no-hoper would become a natural fly-half or a full-back, or a winger of genuine pace would stand before me. So too in the classroom understanding would suddenly break through and the boy was on his way to real achievement.

During a boy's last term in the upper sixth the atmosphere was often magical. Grades A and B in the exams brought telephone calls from parents for a belated application for a higher education course. It was wonderful being in a school which not only encouraged the development of natural talent in the educational process but which also went out of its way to foster individual interests and enthusiasms outside the curriculum. Most of the staff were involved in extracurricular activity of one sort or another – with the orchestra, with the dramatic society, with the science society – and nearly every night of term something would be happening.

For three successive years I was fortunate enough to be appointed a course tutor at a residential seminar run by the Derbyshire Education Authority, when fifty of the most academically gifted pupils in the county were joined by ten teachers selected for the breadth of their talents. There were enough musicians among us to form an orchestra, for example, and concerts – and even once a display of country dancing – were arranged.

Achieving excellence in the classroom and on the sports field was exhilarating despite the long and tiring hours. And those successes benefited me just as much as my students. They drove away the self-doubt from which I had suffered for years and helped me to acquire, at last, some sort of status in my role as teacher. However, administration has always been my Achilles heel; I have always lacked any sense of

efficient organisation and that weakness continues to this day. My wife
looks after me domestically, my company secretary keeps meticulous
order in my business affairs; elsewhere I am just tolerated. The office
staff at school were always chasing me for lost invoices. The headmaster,
Geoff Price, was exasperated by my inefficiency, suffering alternate
bouts of frustration and elation with his head of economics and master-in-charge of rugby. He was chuffed over the examinations and
games results – all those successful Oxbridge candidates from my department, Derbyshire Sevens rugby champions, the best academic results
in the school, both qualitatively and quantitively – but oh, those invoices.
I used to take Geoff to rugby and cricket matches at Headingley, the
directors' box at Nottingham Forest, and so on. So I suppose I made
some amends for my weakness; and anyway my accounts were always
balanced at the end of the year. When I was county treasurer for
Derbyshire schoolboy rugby, Anne, thank goodness, balanced the books.

I find it almost impossible to describe dispassionately my virtues and
many failings as a teacher. But over the years former students have
written to me and some of those letters I have kept. Looking back
through that file, I think these three are the most articulate and present
a reasonably balanced portrait of what I must have been like teaching
the sixth form. The first is from Dean Harper, now an associate lawyer
in London:

'You're in Lower VI Modern TCT,' followed by a sharp intake
of breath, was the first I heard of 'Cec' Thompson on my first
day in the sixth form of Chesterfield School for Boys in September
1983.
    'Yes,' I naively replied.
    'Do you play rugby?'
    'No,' I answered. 'Is that a problem?'
    Another sharp intake of breath was followed by 'You'll see,'

and sniggers from the boys who were already in Lower VI Modern TCT. 'He's tough but fair . . . sometimes,' said another boy. I think he was trying to reassure me and return some colour to my by now ashen face.

With this sort of build-up I really didn't quite know what to expect when you finally entered the form room. The man who walked through the door carrying an attendance register didn't appear too much of an ogre – but I was later to learn that he could be, if provoked.

Not only were you my form master for the two years I was at Chesterfield School but you also taught me macroeconomics, led me through the Oxbridge entrance exam, and became my occasional political sparring partner – arguing, I like to believe, in order to play the devil's advocate rather than out of real disagreement with my political stance.

Modesty was not a quality of yours that I remember. You had had a successful rugby career before 'receiving the calling to teach' (your words) and you were determined that no one would forget it. 'A legend in his own rugby shorts' was how a few boys described you. I can't comment on your rugby career but you were certainly legendary at Chesterfield School. In any school there are always masters who are respected and feared. At Chesterfield you were one of these. A rowdy classroom would immediately settle down to intense study when it was rumoured that you had been spotted wandering the corridors. But you were respected as well as feared: your lessons were not simply a matter of sitting down and taking notes but were much more interactive. A lesson on the economic policy of the 'boom-burst' 1960s could be a bit soporific with the wrong teacher. With you it was often as lively as Prime Minister's Question Time. My political views were known to virtually all the boys and staff in the school; there were other boys with equally strong but opposing views. You would often deliberately provoke a political slanging match in your lessons between me and those other boys. It doesn't take much to get rabid teenage politicians into action. You played the role of Speaker, trying to ensure that all sides were heard. 'Back up your arguments with facts and statistics', you always said, and we did.

What you were doing so successfully was encouraging us to learn the theory you were teaching and apply it to the things we saw happening around us; you enabled us to understand it using the same intellectual tools you were handing out to us. There is no doubt that you helped me develop my raw political conviction into a more coherent form. For that I am grateful to you. But you were also willing to give up your free time to help those who wanted to push themselves a little further academically than the 'A' level course itself allowed. I decided to attempt entrance to Oxbridge and sit the entrance exam. In the two months leading up to that exam, you gave up two evenings a week to teach me privately, often at your home. That showed a dedication virtually unheard of in the state education sector. For that, too, I am very grateful.

As a form-master you were jovial. There were very few boys who did not feel the sharp side of your wit. I did not escape: after an experiment with lightening the colour of my hair I was subjected to weeks of reference to the Golden Boy, the Sun Flower, and Blondie. If you were sensible, you took it in your stride and hoped you would pass on to someone else soon. If you rose to the bait and retaliated you would only succeed in lengthening your period of suffering!

Ostensibly, you are a social snob, dropping the names of famous people you know into any conversation and appearing to place great emphasis on the fact that you lived in the salubrious 'Brookside' area on the west side of the town. But nobody took your jibes seriously, and I always felt that it was not where a boy was at any particular stage in his life that you admired but his determination to climb as high as possible in a chosen area. It was only those boys who had no direction and couldn't be encouraged to be ambitious that you had no time for. Anyone who had a spark of ability was encouraged to make the very best of himself. We often felt we were pushed too hard, but later we understood and appreciated the part you had played in our success.

Michael Toth was another boy I am proud to have helped. His father, who had fled Hungary at the time of the rising, died when Michael was very young, and his mother had to raise three sons alone. There was little money but a lot of pride in that family, and Michael's brothers did very well academically: one got a first-class honours degree in ecology, the other a Ph.D in microbiology. Michael was the black sheep, totally uninterested in academia, or even in his homework; the only thing he had in his favour was that he was strong.

Before he came to Chesterfield School he had never played rugby; soon he was representing first his school, then his county, and finally he was playing for the Three Counties side – Derbyshire, Nottinghamshire and Leicestershire – on a tour of the north of England. He wrote a letter to me in appreciation of what I had done for him:

> The thing which stands out most in my mind about you, Cec, was when I was working and I told you I could not make it for the game on Saturday. Whow! You hit the roof and threw a fit. It was a few weeks after I'd been picked for the Three Counties tour. You said, 'Toth, if you don't play on Saturday, you're off the tour!' I went away thinking you were the lousiest bastard under the sun bar none, but because I believed you meant it, and because you are bigger than me, I popped into work and begged for the day off, telling them that my dog had died and that I was terribly upset. I got on the bus, still resenting the fact that you had made me lose a day's pay. You sat next to me, pulled out a tenner and said, 'If you are short of money this week, I'll make it up to you.' I didn't take the money but I appreciated the thought. I don't know any teacher that would have made such an offer. I thought you were a hard teacher, but also a fair one. Cheers!

Michael never got much else out of school. He left when he was sixteen and got a labouring job. I still see him; he is poor but happy, retaining the zest for life that extract suggests. In complete contrast, the next letter is from Antony Spencer, who certainly did get the most out of his time at Chesterfield School:

I am writing these few words about my perception of you during my time at Chesterfield and as I sit here in Oxford within the walls of an institution which is the end result of the education of which you were an important part, it seems an apt time to write.

My first memory of you, Cec, is just a remaining blur from a pre-admittance introductory guide to the school. I remember already being anxious about the size and apparently high-powered academic standards in the school, compared to what I had experienced before. I was in the room next to yours and remember you taking obvious pride in wearing an academic gown which I thought was by then merely a relic of a bygone system. I guess that exemplified what you were: an anachronism in a system which had moved on and, as such, your approaches were seen as outmoded if not held with a certain quaint fondness. You obviously believed in what could be called a 'human' education system, in which the teacher and pupil have a relationship beyond the simple one-way flow of information; instead, the teacher involved himself in practically the whole development and upbringing of the pupil. If you weren't so committed to spreading your religion of education to normally disadvantaged groups, I could imagine you teaching at one of the top public schools where the headmaster supposedly knows the names of every pupil and each master fondly reminisces about the fathers and elder brothers of new pupils.

Cec, you didn't see yourself as part of the science of education, where a certain required quantity of knowledge is imparted to the pupil who, given the usual amount of intellectual fall-out, remembers this to repeat in rote. Instead, you were a chimera of approaches, none of which gave the impression of being pre-

ordained, but more a feeling of the external manifestations of a
fairly chaotic mind working feverishly, attempting to grasp the
ends of ideas and form them into a coherent explanation of life.
I got the impression that you were teaching by feeling, groping
your way to some ultimate aim which would educate others at
the same time as helping you explain your own particular preoccupation; you were not just teaching us but learning from us as
well. Sometimes, say during a breaktime, you would stare blankly
at the walls or ceiling as if actually trying to piece together a
confused jigsaw of thoughts and feelings.

In fact, Cec, you were completely disorganised in what could
be called mundane organisational matters. If given an article for
distribution to the rest of the class, you would misplace it somewhere in your trademark bulging suitcase, re-finding it a few days
later. However, this was all part of your approach. This took the
form, to the great irritation of your pupils, of keeping a class in
during a lunch-hour, until a particular idea had been drilled into
an otherwise apathetic group of boys. At the other extreme, you
would try to ambush both staff and pupils, by telephoning them
out of the blue and asking them an economics question to keep
them on their toes. It was this lack of acceptance of formalities
which allowed you to give me extra lessons during lunch-breaks
and games periods, resulting in my gaining a place at Oxford.

Really, you know, the best description of your method is 'mental
bullying'. You would not only ask a question, you demanded an
answer, and if a pupil was indifferent you would try to enrage
him, making him passionate enough to reply: this was all part of
the 'human approach'. You inspired strong feelings with these
methods – fierce loyalty and a hatred just as fierce, if shorter lived
– but mostly you inspired respect. You obviously took your work
as a teacher seriously, recalling with pride those students you had
seen rise from humble beginnings to a successful career during
your period of teaching, yet you kept your humour and never
lost your enthusiasm. To some extent this was because of the way

you dismissed mundane reality: you virtually worked in an environment of your own invention, devising a totally fictitious biography for a member of staff or a pupil – gigolo, sex fanatic or drug addict – and maintaining it for years. In this way you were not only a teacher but 'one of the lads', on a par with the pupils. But what really differentiated you from the other teachers, and the pupils, is that you maintained your belief and mission in teaching. Whereas other teachers had become demoralised by their conditions and obsessed with their routines, and most pupils had forgotten their identity in a rigid system, you maintained the source of energy – your desire to spread knowledge as widely and deeply as you possibly could.

I have enjoyed a number of lasting friendships with other sixth-formers who, like Dean Harper and Anthony Spencer, went on to Oxford or Cambridge. Duncan Taylor, a regular member of the Chesterfield 1st XV, was one who went to Oxford and once gave us a marvellous day there, inviting our schoolboy team to play his college at rugby. And another was Chris Harrison, who went to Cambridge to read economics, and once invited Anne and Mark and me for a weekend of punting on the Cam and champagne picnics by the riverside. It all seemed far removed from my Hunslet factory days. But it was important to remember that while I had been labouring there other people, many of them perhaps the parents of those I was now amongst, would have been spending weekends such as this in the same unchanging and idyllic environment.

I find it particularly heartening when boys from really poor homes make a success of their lives. One old boy, who invited me to his posh wedding, wrote that he owed all his successes in life to me. I don't suppose for one moment that that was true, but it was nice to think that he apparently thought it was.

Chapter 12

We all have a skeleton or two in the cupboard. The poorest in our society are subject to the greatest temptations, because they have least to lose as well as most to gain. Those with more comfortable lives have less reason to stray from the straight and narrow. But this does not mean that the former are inferior to the latter.

I have never spoken publicly of my divorce, believing it to be a strictly private matter. But there are other dints in my armour, and I certainly don't want readers to think that I regard myself as saintly, far from it. However, as an observer of human behaviour and character, I suspect the dints just go to show that I am normal. When a marriage fails both parties must share the blame, though not necessarily equally. Were it not for the sterling qualities of my second wife, Anne, it could have happened again.

Since our move to Chesterfield Anne and I had been living at 740 Chatsworth Road which, I have to confess, was a bit of a let-down after Woodsetts. We missed our luxurious kitchen and our magnificent garden. But the house had a lot of character with an attractive front lawn, dry-stone walling and a two-level garden at the back with trees and shrubs and manicured lawns. There was a splendid conservatory, running the whole width of the house, looking on to a garden at the back. In addition to our living-room we now had no less than four bedrooms, from one of which we could look out over the Derbyshire hills behind the house, and there was agricultural land at the front.

Mark had had his first birthday shortly after we arrived in that big house, and at the same time Anne developed disc trouble. We had summoned Anne's aunt, Sally, the moment the trouble started and before she arrived, twenty-four hours later, I had to dash home at the end of each lesson: it was only a ten-to fifteen-minute journey but was pretty disruptive all the same. When Sally arrived she made it clear that she could cope only with Mark's minor requirements. In fact, she could deal with the nappies but I was still the general dogsbody; and she made it clear that she would not be able to cook.

Initially, Anne's treatment was to lie flat on a wooden board. But after several uncomfortable weeks of this she had to go into hospital for a month on traction. Abandoned with Mark and his nappies I was distraught. My time was already fully committed to the department and to rugby, and though we got a home help for a few days there was a more urgent case than ours and she had to leave. Apart from having to dash home during breaks and in the lunch-hour to see how things were going I had to do my marking through the night. My nerves were on edge but I just about managed to stay outwardly calm.

When Mark started school, Anne's back collapsed again. This time Mark and I worked out a strict routine and the headmaster was very helpful in letting me manipulate my school timetable to allow me time to take Mark to and from school. It was a curious experience, all the young mothers plus me in a group, watching our children start their first day at school. I was growing tense, and when Anne had recovered I found what seemed like the release I needed. I began to visit the Terminus, the local pub, after school each Tuesday and Thursday. The Terminus is right outside the school gates, and opening time coincided with the end of rugby training on those evenings. It was great to be able to join that convivial company for an hour or so instead of going straight home to my son and wife, though I loved them both dearly.

Anne hated the way I was coming home later and later. 'I want my husband,' she told me once. 'Can't you see I'm lonely?' I brought her some flowers as a peace token: she gave them back. 'Don't try it on with me, Cecil Thompson! It's you that I want, not flowers. We're a family without a father. I can't take this life any more.'

'Darling, I need a break and a couple of drinks in the Terminus with like-minded friends.' I thought I was being reasonable. 'It's therapeutic. I love you and I love Mark.' Saturday lunchtimes were the same. After the morning match, there would be a few drinks –

and on away days I still called in at the Terminus first. On Friday after school, the staff and the boys' relations could use the school swimming-pool. I would be teaching Mark different styles of swimming and generally having fun with him. Then he too would come with me to the Terminus. It had grown to be almost a second home. I carried on like this for three or four years, then took stock.

I realised that the well-disciplined, healthy sportsman had taken a liking to drink and to the companionship of the other regulars in the bar. All this was undeniably helpful to me but equally selfish towards Anne and I realised too that I was missing so much at home.

So I cut the Terminus out of my life, but not, unfortunately, the booze. I started to take drink home instead. One day, I could see that Anne was not happy with me. 'I would like to have a simple mother and father conversation,' she announced. 'How do you think your son will grow up, always seeing his father with a glass of booze in his hands, any hour of the day?' There were other warnings. One Saturday morning on the rugby field one of my players was slightly concussed. I blew into his eyes to see how severe the effects were. 'I feel a bit woozy, sir,' he said, 'from the whisky fumes on your breath.'

In the same fashion my manageress, Shirley Hogan, told me that my cleaning staff in the various offices around West Cumbria reported that they could always smell booze when I called to see them. The messages were coming loud and clear. I stopped drinking alcohol for eighteen months completely, and then I had a difference of opinion over Mark's education and became once more a regular in the Terminus.

Yet this time I knew it was a mistake, and that there was no therapeutic need for drinking. I had lived without it once, after all. I went to the Hunslet reunion dinner – held annually in a Leeds hotel – and looked around me. Where were the sleek athletes of yesterday? Instead I was surrounded by beer-bellies and sagging muscle. I have always taken pride in my fitness, always kept myself in shape. It was my future I saw around me. I read about Jim Morrison, Jimi Hendrix, George Best, superb talents laid low by indulgence. I had a lovely wife, a wonderful son, a pleasant home, but where would I be in twenty years? I went to a doctor who confirmed the worst. The drink was having its effect: I was going downhill pretty rapidly. And that was it: I haven't touched alcohol now for seven years, and I cannot imagine ever having another drink. Without it I'm extremely happy and oozing with confidence – and it was in order to be all of that that I, like most people, used to want to drink in the first place.

I have said elsewhere that Geoff Price was a traditional headmaster, believing in hard work and self-discipline, a formidable head with a strong streak of authority, but offset with a keen sense of humour. He allowed his senior staff full freedom when that was justified by academic results. I enjoyed this freedom and Geoff was tremendously supportive when one day I found myself in really serious trouble.

A fifth-year student had not handed in his GCSE project. He asked for a few more days but I warned him that the deadline was near at hand for the projects to be posted to an external examiner. When the final day arrived, I spotted him coming into school and asked him, 'Have you brought in your project?' He replied, 'I have forgotten it, sir.' At the same time I saw him grinning at a friend. I swung round to declare my annoyance and must have startled him since he fell to the ground. He reached out with his hand to check his fall and sprained his thumb and wrist in the process. That evening I was summoned to the police station. I was to be arrested for assault, having punched a student to the ground, causing a fractured thumb. I was placed in a small room from 8.00 p.m. to 9.45 p.m. and was interrogated by a policeman who sat at the table in front of me with another at my side. I refused to say anything until I had a legal representative present. I was allowed to telephone a neighbour whose best friend was a lawyer. A lawyer actually lived next door to me but this was to be a very private affair. Eventually a lawyer arrived after I had been waiting for about an hour: it had been awkward for him to leave home at that time of night on the spur of the moment. Anyway, the interrogation then took place and lasted about forty-five minutes, with myself still flanked by the two policemen. I had not had any alcohol for several years but when we left the police station the lawyer and I went to the nearest pub and had a couple of glasses of beer. When I got home I simply could not believe what had happened.

I suspect local politics – an antagonism towards the anomalous position of Chesterfield School – came into the decision to prosecute. The case itself was comparatively simple. A boy's parents took me to court for physical injury to their son, something I did not do. However, the politicking was such that my solicitor felt that we would not get a fair hearing in the local court and asked that the case be tried at the Crown Court at Derby with a barrister to defend me. It would involve a good deal of expenditure and a great deal of inconvenience but such are the wheels of justice. I did not discuss the case at all at school because I was afraid of gossip. Nor did I discuss it with Anne because I saw no reason why she should worry too; indeed, she did not know about the case at all until the day before each court hearing.

Particularly distressing was the attitude of my employers, the local education committee. In a one-sentence letter they told me that, in the event of my losing the case, I would be dismissed. It was frightening to see the labour of a lifetime put in jeopardy by one boy's fabrications.

Meanwhile, I was notified by the education authority that I must not talk to the boy and he had to be transferred from my class to another class within my department. It seemed as though I had been found guilty before any formal judgement had been passed. The boy in question further accused me, weeks after the original accusation, of trying to reverse my car into him with the intention of injuring him. This incident was also brought to the attention of the education authority and I was instructed to report to the headmaster's office to defend myself in the presence of an education officer. It seemed as though I was being victimised, but I kept cool and went through the formalities. Once again, witnesses were apparently available to support the boy. A sixth-form lesson was disrupted while I went through this mock court and further restrictions were placed on me. I really was being treated as though I were a criminal. Only Geoff Price and my two lawyers were my confidants. Whatever the prosecution said had happened was their affair.

Fortunately, I was able to remain comparatively philosophical about it all. I went about my life mechanically, never going to parties, absorbing myself in school work, leaving and arriving punctually at the official school hours and generally leading a quiet domestic exist-ence.

The local magistrates' court was a dreadful experience and, once again, I had to miss lessons. My cleaning company is contracted to clean the court rooms at Workington and Whitehaven, where opulent facilities are provided. So I knew at first hand the sort of disgusting filth that is left behind in the waiting-room and that anything that can be unscrewed is stolen. When it was my turn to enter the dock, I was wearing a sheepskin coat as the morning was intensely cold. I had my hands in my coat pockets. I was ordered to take my hands out of my pockets. I obeyed instantly and was overcome with apprehension. Was this some instinctive reaction from my paternal ancestors' slave days? But, in a cold sober afterthought, I reflected on my citizen's rights. In the land of my birth had I done something to lose those rights? Why was I being subjected to this humiliation? But I suppose some people find satisfaction in inflicting this sort of sickening cruelty on others. The whole affair was degrading beyond belief, all because of a school project which was four weeks late and several broken promises.

My case was duly transferred to the Derby Crown Court and the hearing was fixed for six weeks later. Another whole day would be spent away from school for me and the allegedly assaulted boy and his five witnesses. After my appearance in the local magistrates' court, the following headline was blazed across the local paper to humiliate me further:

CHESTERFIELD SCHOOLMASTER IN COURT OVER ALLEGED ASSAULT ON LOCAL SCHOOLBOY

This whole sorrowful series of events had begun in September, the

Crown Court hearing was down for March, and the cost to me of
those six months of anxiety was incalculable. My flamboyance disappeared; I lived a completely monastic life. In some ways it was
wonderful because being encased in a cocoon has its advantages. But
I was aloof to everyone, monosyllabic, back to my teenage days, in fact,
though wiser and more self-possessed. As the weeks dragged by, I even
began to be unconcerned about the outcome of the case. I believe in
my natural goodness, I kept saying. I can be surrounded by wretchedness
but there is no hate, no aggression, no brutality within me, only dignity
and self-respect. Why should anyone want to harm me?

My lawyers worked hard on my behalf and I had regularly to visit
my barrister's chambers in Nottingham and my solicitor's home in
Chesterfield. Between us we structured my case and we rehearsed it
thoroughly. I have to say that my solicitor was brilliant all the way
through, paying great attention to detail. I was truly grateful to him;
he made the case for the barrister a comparatively simple matter of
fabricated evidence by the prosecution. On the day of the Crown
Court hearing my headmaster turned up in case he could be of any
help to me and the sight of him reassured me. He knew I was innocent
but that alone would not necessarily carry the day for me.

I had to be at Derby at 9.30 a.m. for the trial to begin at 11.00 a.m.
During the morning our party was approached by the prosecution's
lawyer for a settlement out of court. We decided that that would not
clear my honour as a schoolmaster, and it was my integrity that was
at stake. It was a risk I was prepared to take, believing that truth would
win through in the end.

Standing in the dock with a policeman on either side of me, it
seemed as though I were in a film. To support my case I had received
a number of character references, from old boys, from headmasters,
parents, the secretary-general of the Rugby Football League, the chairman of Workington Town. These were photocopied and handed round
the court officials. It was some consolation to know that, though I
would be treated like a common criminal if I lost, I still had the respect
of those whom I respected. My current headmaster, Geoffrey Price,

wrote that Mr Cecil Thompson 'has worked hard and very successfully
in the pursuit of excellence for the boys in his charge. His results in
examination have been sound and very many boys have good reason
to be thankful that he demanded from them sincere effort and rigorous
study. He is a more than competent teacher, well liked, hard working
and with real care for his pupils.'

I was surprised the head had noticed so much. 'Outside the classroom,'
he continued, 'Mr Thompson has given freely of his time, energies
and expertise. He took over the school rugby and made it a most
successful sport; the education authority recognised his ability when
they invited him to be a course tutor for county seminars in economics.
He is always ready to assist in school functions, students' concerts, staff
evenings and parents association events.' It was upsetting to read about
myself in the past tense like this, but nice to know that I was appreciated.
'In my dealings with Mr Thompson,' the headmaster concluded, 'he
has demonstrated to me that he is affable and pleasant, willing to help
and to put himself out to be of assistance. He has shown me determination in all he does. I have found him to be honest, straightforward,
sincere and most genuinely interested in getting along with his fellow
men.' That was pretty impressive but would it help to convince the
court?

David Oxley was equally flattering. 'I am secretary-general of the
Rugby Football League,' he wrote. 'I have known Mr Cecil Thompson
for many years. He was a professional Rugby League player for over
fifteen years, and records reveal that he was never once dismissed from
the field of play nor ever cautioned for foul play at any time during
his career. I have had the privilege of watching Mr Thompson play
rugby on numerous occasions. I never once saw him commit an act
of foul play or violence on the field, despite the fact that his superb
skills and, on occasions, his colour, made him a target for opposition
players.' Once again, it came as a pleasant surprise that anyone else
had noticed.

Finally, there was a letter from my old chairman at Workington,
my friend Tom Mitchell, a director of the club for forty years and a

past chairman of the Rugby League Council, who also made much of my disciplinary record. 'Mr Cecil Thompson played seven seasons as a forward for Workington. During that time, never once was he dismissed from the field of play. Not only that, but I cannot recall a single instance of loss of composure or any retaliatory act in the whole of his playing career. In my opinion, he is one of that diminishing breed of gentlemanly players, not only on the field but off it too, a model of sportsmanship.'

Yet none of these people had been in school at the time of the alleged incident and ranged against me were the boy and the boy's friends who had been.

Were the boys enjoying this fantasy? At least it was better than being at school. But soon, as cross-examination got under way, they began to realise the folly of their trickery. There was little harmony between the pieces of evidence they had prepared. When, under pressure, they cracked and lost their tempers, their stories broke down and it became obvious that these so-called witnesses had made up their evidence. So a bunch of idle students were seen to have been trying to mock their industrious teacher. When the time came for me to be cross-examined I recalled the series of events which had led up to the alleged assault. The judge seemed to be more interested in how I had become a schoolmaster. I briefly summarised my life from orphanage to classroom and I think he was impressed by my down-to-earth endeavours, raising myself from manual labourer to pedagogue. He enquired, 'How did you manage financially?' 'By cleaning windows,' I replied. My character references endorsed my mild nature and my self-discipline.

So I had won. But it was disillusioning to learn how fragile was the crown I had earned for all my years of endeavour, how easily it could all have been swept away. After the trauma of the court case, it was some consolation to be made a housemaster in the same academic year. The housemaster of the house in question, Steve Poulton, had undertaken the arduous role of overseeing the school timetable, felt he could not do both jobs, and had recommended me to take his place; and the headmaster approved.

A not dissimilar affair to the alleged assault, in its unfairness if not its gravity, occurred when an incompetent teacher joined my department who, over several years, completed only two-thirds of the contracted attendance time. I tried in vain to appeal to the teacher by kindness, charm, hospitality in my home, by using the whole range of persuasion in my armoury for better attendance, punctuality, not to leave the classroom during lessons, and to set and mark homework conscientiously. I asked the teacher for lessons to be used for instruction and not for relating idle gossip, and in collaboration with the headmaster I kept a file of parents' complaints. However, my entirely justifiable accusations were thought to be harassment and were reported to a trade union official. Again, I was ordered to attend a mock trial to defend myself; it seemed that I was jeopardising my career and that it was I who was the guilty party. Of course the issue was really about parents getting a fair deal for their sons but, somehow, it was I who was thought to be in the wrong. I was caught in those shark-infested waters between the right and left wings of local politics and we were drifting miles away from the simple wish to improve a student's mind and his capacity to learn.

I was at Chesterfield Grammar School for seventeen years. Then in 1991, coinciding with my retirement and, after a bitter dog fight between the school governors and the local education authority which had lasted nearly a decade, the school closed its doors after 397 years to become fully comprehensive. Those last years were bizarre. After such a long and distinguished history, a school cannot suddenly change its ethos. The townsfolk, students, staff and old boys still referred to the beloved institution as the grammar school. The rugby teams retained their song, 'Chesterfield Grammar School Are We', which they sang proudly in the dressing-room after each match, win or lose. And the students continued to follow the hard road of mountains of homework and tough internal exams.

I was deeply impressed by the quality and dedication of the staff during my time at the school. And I believe I was able to broaden the horizon of the students I taught while at the same time becoming, I hope, a more enlightened person myself. The school's main aim always was not to produce high flyers but to encourage youngsters to spread their wings. To be a member of a team producing such a service to the community and to the nation at large was a privilege. A school which has helped to shape the lives of boys for almost four centuries made me feel as if I too was part of history.

Geoffrey Price, the headmaster, was in the driving seat for twenty-four years, from 1968 to within a term of the school's closure. He defended its traditions to the end, battling in vain to keep the school as it was in an opt-out struggle. His boast was that employers would say, 'If he went to Chesterfield Boys School, that's good enough for me.' He believed in things that are anathema in today's system, for example, his belief in the pursuit of excellence in competition with others. He was the school's longest serving head and as a traditionalist he held his ground over things like haircuts, dress and discipline. The school left its imprint on nearly all of us, certainly on me. My friendships with the boys and the staff remain just as strong today as they were then and just as strong as the links I forged with my mates at Hunslet and Workington all those years ago.

Frictions in the school were invariably solved through reason and by discussion. Treating students in an adult manner always pays dividends. Since no less than a quarter of the school population were sixth-formers, a mature atmosphere prevailed. Becoming a head of department obviously gave me much greater confidence in myself. Being a father and having a more responsible position in the school and in the community, some sense of stability entered my life for the first time.

All in all, it was a joyful experience to be at Chesterfield for those seventeen years although I have never worked so hard in all my life. Real wealth to me is the ability to say no to work I don't want to do and to be able to travel every summer to wherever I want to go. So

I ended my career as a teacher a much wealthier person in more ways than money can bring.

Always on the move from my middle-class home and occupation in Chesterfield to my working-class business in Cumbria, and to Shrewsbury School's social gatherings, when Mark was at school there, I sometimes received some pretty odd shocks. My social acrobatics were even more spectacular on my visits to Harrow when Maloney was on the staff. So many generations – grandfathers and fathers and sons and uncles and cousins – had been to Harrow that all the boys had become stereotyped like penguins. On the other hand, Eton provided a moving experience for me when one of my sixth-formers won a scholarship. His family could not even afford a telephone. Sheer ability and total commitment produced this outstanding result. And it was also proof that Eton was definitely not 'exclusive', sitting at the top of that strange pyramid, the British class structure.

Shrewsbury, Harrow, Eton – what a far cry from those tall mill chimneys which surrounded the Barley Mow ground at Bramley in that now far-distant works competition at the start of my rugby career; from that sweltering bakery in Meanwood Road with the trams grinding past; and from the working-class school at Dinnington where I began my years of teaching. But, however elevated may have been the ledge on which I found myself eventually, I still bear some of the scars, both physical and psychological, from my window-cleaning round and from that horrendous game when Pitchford's stiff-arm tackle broke my nose and our winning streak at The Watersheddings. It has been a tough and bloody road all right. But, all in all, I would not have had it otherwise.

PART 5

REFLECTING

Chapter 13

On Friday, 22 July 1994, in company with the Speaker of the House of Commons, Betty Boothroyd; Raymond Seitz, the retiring US Ambassador; Margaret Atwood, the novelist; Chief Eleazar Chukwuremaka Anyaoku; and a cluster of distinguished scientists, I received the degree of Master of Arts *in honoris causa* from the Chancellor of Leeds University, HRH the Duchess of Kent. I have no idea why the Chancellor's Court should have chosen to honour me in this way but they did and my honorary degree has become my most precious possession. For me it symbolises the end – and what a glorious end – of my search for some sort of balanced life.

Though teaching has certainly been at the centre of my affairs for the last twenty-five years, it has never been my only concern. In many ways, as I have explained elsewhere, my entrepreneurial activity with my cleaning company has been equally important, in many ways more important, since my struggle for a degree and the whole of my teaching career would never have happened without the money my company brought in. And just as the success of my company has to some extent sprung from my status as a local rugby hero, so my rugby career might have been very different had I not had first to endure the iron discipline of hard manual work as a labourer. So the circle has been joined.

Making money for its own sake has never appealed to me but I know that the modest amounts of money I have made have enabled me to enjoy a balanced life, certainly a varied one, and I know for sure that a balanced life is better than a blinkered one. I once heard Sir Roger Bannister explain that though the four-minute mile was important to him – it had made him a household name after all – his career as a neurologist, and his interest in music and the arts, mattered to him a good deal more. I admire – and in my own way try to emulate – that balance between intellectual interests, athletic skills and aesthetics. Another hero of mine, J. P. R. Williams, was similarly well rounded, being not only a wizard of Welsh Rugby Union but also a doctor of medicine with a passion for music. And another who refuses to be pigeonholed, and whom I admire greatly, is Seb Coe, who has moved successfully from athletics to politics, acquiring a degree along the way.

In Britain, most of those who achieve this well-rounded, balanced life are middle-class boys and girls who have enjoyed an expensive education and the privilege of a stable, usually monied, home life. In marked contrast stand my own family. Of the boys, all three of us were six-footers and well proportioned. I did not meet Robert Cyril, my eldest brother, born in 1921, until I was about fourteen. He was like a film star in those days, with delicate facial features, and always impeccably dressed. Whatever he owned he always maintained in perfect order. I looked upon him as some kind of hero, particularly as the reason he had come to our home in Leeds in 1940 or 1941 was to enlist. He joined the Royal Warwickshire Regiment and was then posted to the 14th Army in Burma with the York & Lancaster Regiment for practically the whole of the war.

After the war he married Blanche Lee, a vivacious blonde girl from the north-east, and with his demob money opened a cobbler's shop in a poor neighbourhood of Leeds. Within three years they had had two children and it was a hard life. He needed money to feed and clothe his family and he needed to get that money off his customers. Friday was national pay day for the working man and each Friday would see Bob tramping round the neighbourhood with the repaired footwear, trying to get paid. This state of affairs wore him out. In the end he decided to close his shop and went down the mines where there was a big demand for labour and a guaranteed weekly wage. Robert and Blanche had four children, three boys and one girl. Sadly, the marriage did not last and they were divorced in the early 1960s. Blanche now lives near Haworth in the Brontë country, close to her daughter Brenda. After the divorce Bob married again and still lives in Leeds.

Years of underground work in wet conditions eventually took their toll on Bob. He accepted early retirement and had to have operations for two artificial hips. He remains abundantly cheerful but his mobility is sadly limited these days, and his potential was never developed.

I first met my other brother, Aubrey, younger than Bob, in similar circumstances. He had been working on a farm near Worcester before coming home to Leeds to enlist in 1943. He joined the RAF, and after demobilisation he entered and won a talent competition with the BBC. He was the only artistic one in the family, being quite an accomplished singer; in fact he was a smaller edition of Paul Robeson with his deep bass voice. Aubrey was never a sportsman but was an extremely versatile musician. All my family were pretty quiet and reserved and Aubrey was the most reserved. For two or three years he toured the clubs in the north of England but after a time won a contract as a night club manager in Australia. He adored Australia and loved the people and way of life. Then he was involved in a serious road accident.

For many years nothing was heard from him. Just when he seemed to have a gilded career ahead of him, he disappeared into oblivion. Then, suddenly, out of the blue, I received this letter from him in 1972, just after my own serious car crash:

> Apologies (sincerely) for not having written before now. Very disturbed at hearing of your unfortunate accident and trust you recover very quickly. Explanation of incommunicado: brain damage caused through car accident several years ago. Difficult to explain full effects except that I appear to live in a dream world.
>
> I have had to relinquish my position as a club manager and now drive a delivery truck. Lost all sense of smell and taste and have very little emotional feelings. Perhaps an exchange of correspondence might help to produce a recuperative situation. This letter, I must say, comes about through the persistent wrangling of a

'taffy' – surname escapes me – whom I met last Christmas. He informed me of your accident. Often while driving I think of you and swear to you that on arrival home I will write, but immediately I arrive home my mind goes dead. Occasionally light breaks through as today, and hence the letter.

Will write more fully if possible within a day or two and, once again, trust you recover speedily, and with no recurring damage.

Yours very sincerely, Aub

I replied immediately and have written numerous times since but have heard nothing more.

Aubrey was the brightest of us. He was doubly gifted: he had the vision to move away from home to find an outlet for his talents, as our father had done, and he had the good sense to direct himself along one particular path, developing his musical abilities as he went along. Yet how much more might he have achieved had he been groomed from childhood?

I first met my only sister, Linda, in Leeds in 1938 when, at the age of twelve, I left my orphanage in Tynemouth. She was attractive and slim, and had a beautiful disposition. She worked as a machinist in a textile factory and helped in the family bakery in the evenings. She was an uncomplicated person, accepted life as it unfolded and was always a joy to be with. I was surprised as well as delighted when, shortly after our mother died, she opened up her own confectionery shop. She had married Eric Pearson, a local man, charming and intelligent, and the two of them ran the business together.

Like me, Linda showed an unexpected entrepreneurial flair, and the success of the business allowed her and Eric to make a delightful home for themselves in Leeds, in Carr Manor Drive, where Eric still lives. Then came the terrible news that Linda, like our mother, had developed cancer. Anne, Mark and I visited her nearly every week during the last eighteen months of her life. It was heartbreaking to see this beautiful, generous, bubbling person struggling against all odds to stay with us. Slowly we saw her losing the battle. Her lovely features gradually disintegrated, though she remained cheerful to the end. Sadly, Eric had then to sell the business and he now works in his brother's tailoring firm.

The story of my siblings is not particularly unusual, but that makes it no less sad. The thing that distresses me most is that so much potential was wasted, for all four of us would have benefited from firmer direction earlier in our lives. That was certainly not my mother's fault. When I reflect on the terrible months of 1926, when my father died, I cannot find words to express the suffering she must have endured. How distraught she must have been, suddenly to be the widow of a black man she loved so deeply, pregnant with a brown child and already the mother of three other brown children. I understand completely that she had no alternative but to scatter her seed and to pray that one day they would somehow come together again, but the agony of it must have been almost unendurable.

So her children grew up with no strong family ties. I was a stranger to my mother when occasionally she came to see me in Warminster, and doubtless my brothers felt the same. When the four of us were sometimes reunited in wartime we met as strangers.

Later, when my mother married again and started to build up her confectionery business with her new husband, Edwin, I found it difficult to establish any meaningful relationship with her in those cramped rooms at 159 Meanwood Road. Edwin was struggling to make a success of the business in the sweltering bakehouse and my mother had customers to serve in the shop as well as a shy, inarticulate and rather stupid boy to look after, who was drifting from job to meaningless job. And she must have been well aware that a single room in a tiny attic was hardly the place for a teenage boy and a teenage girl to grow up in together. It was certainly an impossible place for her to develop any meaningful discussions with me, even if the inarticulate boy had been able to find some words.

So for most of her adult life my mother knew only suffering. Flo and Bill were a love match and the strength of their love must have been immense to enable them to face the problems they would have had to contend with during their courtship and marriage. It would not have been all that easy for a black journeyman painter to earn a living in Leeds and it would have been more difficult still in Durham, though Florence, as a local girl, among her own people, might have found things easier there. In Leeds, settled in an alien community, it must have been very difficult indeed for her with her black husband and brown children – three piccaninnies – living among strangers.

My mother had never known the luxury of choice with regard to clothes, food, accommodation, holidays. But she knew my father's love. Then suddenly, abruptly, the engine of her life stopped. Bill was dead. She had lost everything – her husband, her home and her children, never to be reunited for over a decade and then in a strange home, the Meanwood Road bakery. And was that really home?

Then, once reunited, the children were scattered again, Bob to Burma, Aubrey to a RAF base near Lincoln, Cecil to the Far East as a stoker in the navy. But my mother endured it all, even the cancer that killed her, with dignity and calm. I never heard her complain and she suffered excruciating pain in silence. She was never roused to anger and I never heard her speak aggressively to anyone. She always carried herself proudly and had a lordly eye, but an eye offset by quite exceptional, deprecating modesty. Now, at a distance of nearly half a century, I have learned to love her deeply.

The closest surviving member of my family is undoubtedly my cousin Joan, a friend for life if ever there was one. Joan is the only child of my mother's younger sister, Elisabeth, who married Leslie Binks in Leeds in 1932. Joan emigrated to Canada in her late teens, married a delightful Finn called Eric and has lived most of her life in Hamilton beside the shores of Lake Ontario.

Joan and I have always enjoyed a close and loving relationship, certainly closer than anything I experienced with my own brothers, perhaps because we both spent our school and teenage years in Leeds. Over the years, we have written volumes of letters to each other and have crossed the Atlantic many times to see each other. And we share an astonishing gift of telepathic thought-transference.

17. My father in 1919 with my mother's parents. The two children are my mother's sister and brother

18. Aged two, with my mother

19 (top left). My brother Bob in the uniform of the York & Lancaster Regt.

20 (top right). My brother Aubrey in RAF uniform

21 (left). My much-loved sister Linda before she was married

22. In Portsmouth, as a Royal Navy recruit, 1944, with two of my pals

23. My wedding day, 1964. *Left to right:* my brother Bob, myself, Anne, who stood rocklike beside me during my long struggle to educate myself, my father-in-law George Taylor and Anne's stepsister Patricia Taylor

24. After graduating with Honours at Leeds University, 1968, I had to face the television cameras, out in force, wearing my mortar-board and holding my Great Britain Rugby League cap. Then I went back to Cumbria to get on with my window-cleaning

25. With Geoffrey Price, headmaster of Chesterfield Grammar School for twenty-three years, and a loyal friend during my years in the school

26. My successes as coach of the Chesterfield Grammar School rugby XV were almost as spectacular as my department's examination results. The first team were Derbyshire Under-19 champions in the 1977–78 season

27. My 1983 form at Chesterfield, which I was especially proud to teach. Dean Harper, whose letter to me is published on page 154, is in the front row, second from the left

28. Our son Mark, aged six, ponders his next move. He was the youngest competitor in an Under-9s tournament

29. With Neil Kinnock, then the Leader of the Opposition, and his wife Glenys, at Wembley stadium after the 1991 Challenge Cup final. Anne is on the right of the picture and next to me is our friend Alexandra Pascoe. My old mate and Town player Andy Key is peering over Neil Kinnock's shoulder

30. With Tom Mitchell, chairman of Workington Town when I was a player there, and a good friend in those far-off days

31. A rare photograph of our friend Donna Carter, in Port of Spain, Trinidad, 1989. She is at the top of the table with a friend; Mark and I are on the right

32. One of my favourite photographs of Anne,
taken during the same visit to Port of Spain, 1989

33. Awarded an honorary degree for services to the community by HRH the Duchess
of Kent, Chancellor of Leeds University, in July 1994.
It was a day I shall never forget

Joan's friendship, consoling in times of stress, joyful at the best of times, has always been wise and balanced, and the practical support she and Eric and their two sons have always given me has provided solid rocks of comfort during my sometimes turbulent life.

In contrast to my family sit the silver-spooners. Starting from positions of relative privilege and given plenty of opportunities when young, they have obvious advantages over children of the working-class. So my son Mark, now himself a silver-spooner, will succeed with comparative ease, I hope, where I have always struggled. At least Mark's life will not be haunted, as mine was, by the fear of being exposed as a member of the under-class with pretensions above his station.

At times, when he was younger, he must have been disturbed by his parents' rather rocky relationship, but now all three of us enjoy each other's company. Mark shows a bemused interest in my frugal background, otherwise he is aloof to it, stemming from his public school and university education. Anne would have liked him to go to a state school but I was the one not wanting him to experience the slightest trauma on ethnic grounds. It is said that while money does not guarantee happiness, it does allow unhappiness to be endured more easily.

I found it immensely difficult at first to adjust to being a teacher: in fact I am not sure that I ever did adjust. The students would say, 'You're not like other members of the staff, sir.' The huge differences in lifestyle hit me when Mark moved to a private school. My very first parent-staff meeting was marked by having to choose between the red and the white wine! I kept quiet in case I made a fool of myself, though Anne and Mark felt quite at home since Anne had been a professional person all her working life. On the way home after such occasions I would reflect on my days at Leeds – the under-class as opposed to the upper-middle-class. I was often asked if I was a 'medic'. 'No, education,' I replied. That would suffice to cover my status since I might even be a university lecturer. I accepted this new awareness with calmness and dignity. After a while I blended in socially with these people, but I was still astonished at the comparison of their lifestyle with those of my workforce in Cumbria, now rapidly expanding.

Mark's school, Shrewsbury, lies in the Midlands belt, away from all those public schools in southern England. Renowned for its rowing, Shrewsbury still boasts the conservative dress of its Regatta Day – blazers, white trousers, boaters, club ties. Indeed, I shall never forget our first Regatta Day: the sun blazing from a clear blue sky; girls in summer dresses and floppy hats; Anne enraptured by it all; and the three of us, Anne and Mark and me, strolling by the Severn as it flowed through acres of playing fields and by one of the finest cricket grounds in the country. There was no doubting that Mark was at a civilised school. We had had a look at several before settling on Shrewsbury. If I thought Giggleswick was magnificent, Shrewsbury's setting is Utopia, and its academic standards outstanding.

Mark's private education has given him tremendous confidence, and I envy him that. There has never been a moment's concern about the colour of his skin: racism has never been an issue. In fact, Mark and I never seem to have spoken nor feel the need to speak about colour. I remember reading a Mark Twain book to him when he was a boy and coming across the word 'nigger'; I stopped reading there and then and vowed that Mark would never suffer the taunts that I had sometimes endured. Sammy Davis Junior in his autobiography says that he wishes his father had not been so protective of him when he was young because the shock of encountering naked racism, when he joined the army, was almost too much to bear. This may well be so. On the other hand, I did not want Mark to encounter racial discrimination or hate at too early an age. Now he is twenty-one and has not had to endure much, if any, prejudice, and for that I can thank his private education.

I can also thank Shrewsbury for giving him his many friends, and the social graces which evaded me during my working-class upbringing. Indeed, Mark's social life, with its skiing, its sailing and its parties, seems utterly wonderful, and in a curious way has even improved my life, because Shrewsbury has had me rubbing shoulders with educated people well above my normal social level. And we have never experienced snobbery of any sort.

So Mark has acquired *savoir faire* but has never showed more than a passing interest in sport. Nor has he any academic ambitions. I had my eyes on a place in an Oxbridge college for him, but I have had to accept that he shows little of my enthusiasm for a university education. I think it is really just a bit of a chore for him: just somewhere to go to pass the necessary exams for a necessary job. Mark has never won a prize at school, was never made a prefect, never became captain of any sport. On the other hand, he has never been ridiculed, made to feel inferior. His expensive education may not have brought the advantages I dreamed of for him but it has given him a social poise which more than compensates for the disadvantage of being a non-white in modern Britain.

Of course racial tension in a given community is not always black against white. In Africa, for example, it is more often than not between tribes or between Asians and the poor black Africans whom they employ or used to employ on their estates. Similarly in Europe, the persecution of the Jews has nothing to do with skin colour. For obvious reasons, when I was growing up or during my years as a manual labourer after the war, I was not really aware of the Jewish community in Leeds. It was only when I returned to live there during the four years I was at university that I felt an affinity between Jews and black people. The Jews had been oppressed for 2,000 years, whereas the huge exodus of black slavery from Africa lasted for barely 350 years. Down the centuries the Jews have been endlessly persecuted and from time to time deprived of everything except their belief in themselves. For their stoicism I admire them greatly.

But Britain does have a serious black/white problem today. A recent

BBC programme illustrated dramatically the degree of racism that exists in this country. Two BBC reporters were given hidden cameras and set loose in Bristol. They looked for accommodation, applied for jobs, tried to join clubs. They were both aged twenty-three, were both graduates, both presentable and pleasant young men. The only difference was that one was white and the other black. The results of their investigation, the outright discrimination the black reporter encountered, represents everyday life in Bristol, and in Britain generally, for most black people today. And it is a terrible fact that nearly 9,000 reported incidents of racial violence took place in Britain in 1993, the total number of unreported incidents perhaps as high as 100,000.

It is almost impossible for a white person to know what it is like to be black in a white society, much less to have felt the pain of discrimination and prejudice. But I once met a white woman who understood. It was a curious situation.

Anne, who at the time was the president of the Chesterfield Soroptomists, attended their international conference in Nottingham. We were about to celebrate our silver wedding with a holiday in Trinidad and Tobago, land of my father's birth, so she was naturally delighted to meet a Trinidadian and duly invited this lady, Donna Carter, to our home for the weekend. We talked into the early hours; then Anne went to bed.

After Anne had gone, I felt free to ask a question that had been troubling me. 'How come you are white?' She smiled as she explained, in her rich West Indian accent, 'My mother was a Carib, my father was French, my colour was a toss-up.' Donna is a respected intellectual in Trinidad and Tobago, involved in a tremendous amount of high-profile social work on the islands. 'At home I am a VIP,' she said. 'I was horrified to find a change of attitude towards me from the moment I arrived in the UK. The taxi driver spoke to me in a contemptuous manner. And I was patronised by others. I am told it is my accent.'

If I look back on my educational development there are certain lessons to be learned. There is general agreement that the first few years of life are the most important in establishing the kind of adult into which a child will grow. However, there is considerable dispute about how much of that adult is the result of his upbringing and how much was there from birth. Is IQ inherited? Or is it influenced by early environment? Or is there some element of both?

However, no one disputes that children from working-class homes perform less well in education than those from the middle classes. According to UCCA, it is a fact that the middle classes have better trained minds, a wider vocabulary and are generally more articulate.

At Leeds, I found nearly all aspects of my university life extremely stimulating. One of the great bonuses were the discussions, the exchanges of ideas, the debates. All aspects of society existed within the campus: theatre, music, media, politics, religion, sport; there was something for everyone. But still something nagged within me and has never left me: my discomfort on social grounds. Is this because I am black or because I was born into the under-class?

Commonsense tells me that it is almost certainly the latter, my upbringing not my colour, though obviously a sensitive black boy growing up in a white society will almost certainly believe that his feelings of inferiority, if he has such feelings, are due in some way to his different colour. After all, my teenage years were spent immediately before and after the Second World War, long before the massive influx of black Commonwealth citizens. The vast numbers of them have caused a sense of insecurity, of unease, leading in many cases to hatred, on the part of white citizens, especially in the outer suburbs of London and in the great industrial centres of the north.

However, except for the hurtful insults of other teenagers, I have very rarely been subjected to any racial abuse by white people – simply to superstition, ignorance and their fear of the unknown, the sort of superstition in Hollywood Tarzan films which showed blacks as cannibals: 'If you don't behave I'll send you to a black man who will gobble you up.'

Later, as a rugby player, I was accepted in Cumbrian society as being no different from the white people around. But away from those surroundings, I have to say that I was sometimes made to feel that I was 'just a black man' and, moreover, at the worst of times, a black man who had made it with a white woman. Now I am forty years older, reasonably well educated, and have become a good deal more streetwise than I was. But occasionally, even now, against all commonsense, I still sometimes believe that it is my colour that makes me feel ill at ease in white society.

Chapter 14

As the reader must know only too well by now, I am always reflecting on the extent to which the game of Rugby League has fashioned my life, directing me down some pretty unexpected paths from one year to the next. My achievements – such as they are – owe so much to the game that its continuing popularity as a spectator sport means a lot to me. In recent years the game has had millions of pounds poured into it through television fees and sponsorship, the latter mainly from tobacco companies and breweries. To a large extent this has been due to the high profile won for the game through the skilful promotion efforts of people such as David Oxley, who retired in 1993 as chief executive, and David Howes, the League's former public relations officer. But now in 1995, as successive recessions have bitten into society, sponsorship money is much harder to come by; gates in some clubs have fallen sharply, and at best have remained static throughout the game; and as the leading players demand, and often receive, wages that the clubs concerned cannot afford, but equally cannot afford not to pay – or so they believe – the structure of the game in England has been put at hazard.

It is interesting to compare a player's wages in my day (the 1950s) with those of stars such as David Watkins (in the 1960s and 1970s) and Alan Tait, now the Leeds full-back (in the 1990s). At Hunslet, we were paid £8 for a win and £5 for a loss. I signed for the club for life for a fee of £250. That was a pretty minuscule sum but was probably fair enough. I had no track record and if I failed to make the grade there would be no headaches on either side.

After I had retired, Brian Snape, the chairman of Salford, transformed the image of the game. He was a visionary, an innovator with an analytical mind. His signing of David Watkins from Welsh Rugby

Union on 19 October 1967 for a then record fee of £10,000 plus a further £1,000 at the start of each of the succeeding five seasons was startling, revolutionary, and began an ever increasing wages spiral. By the end of 1993 the All Blacks wing, Va'aiga Tuigamala, is said to have received £440,000, spread over three years, to play for Wigan on a four-year contract; when Martin Offiah was transferred from Widnes to Wigan in 1992, after long drawn-out negotiations, Offiah was said to be earning £120,000 a year in wages and endorsements. When Widnes signed the great Welsh Rugby Union star, Jonathan Davies, in 1991, he was said to have agreed to accept a contract worth £240,000, spread over three years, in addition to payments of £220 for a win and £60 for a loss. Scott Gibbs, the Wales and British Lions three-quarter, is the latest Rugby Union star to have gone north, signing a five-year contract with St Helens in April 1994 for a reported fee of £250,000.

Compared to the start of my playing days with Hunslet, when few players had a car, and even a telephone at home was a rarity, a player draws his income today from three main sources: first, from the contract signed at the beginning of his League career, usually negotiated by an agent who takes a commission of around 15 per cent; second, from match fees: at Leeds, in 1993–94, the match fees were said to be £330 for a win and £100 for a loss; and third, from bonuses for special games: in the first round of the 1993–94 Challenge Cup, for example, it was reported that the Leeds players would each receive £500 for a win. If Leeds went all the way to Wembley and won, it was said that each player would earn approximately £15,000 to £20,000. Wigan were thought to have received £11,000 per player for the 1993 final alone. All this is a far cry from my day. In 1958, for the Workington v. Wigan final at Wembley, each of the Workington side received £100 for playing and merely a promise of generosity from our late parsimonious chairman, Mr Graves, if we won.

Later in my career at Workington, my winning pay was £15 and losing pay £8. My transfer from Hunslet to Workington gave me no signing-on fee, only a verbal 'thank you' for the efforts I had put into

Hunslet. Now some players are thought to receive 10 per cent of their transfer fee. However, at Workington, mainly due to my local star status, I was able to develop my window-cleaning business. With that money and with what I was earning from my weekly articles on the game I was able gradually to bank some money.

If the Rugby Football League introduces a cap on players' wages (perhaps linked in some way with gate receipts), I will be among the first to applaud. Alternatively, a straight levy could be imposed on gate receipts, which would not only act as a brake on players' wages, and on the high cost of importing players and coaches from Australia and New Zealand, but would also create a reserve of money to be used for the benefit of all clubs in the championship. There is no doubt that clubs are spending more than they can afford and the game will gradually fall into ruin if disciplines of this sort are not imposed.

Money must be spent on ground improvements. Many stadiums now look sad and ill-cared-for, some almost derelict. The implement-ation of the Taylor Report, however necessary from the point of view of safety, has eaten up important reserves of cash which would have been spent on more mundane facilities for the fans; now those facilities are long overdue. And not only are the stands, the lavatories, the refreshment areas and so on drab and uninviting on many grounds but the playing surface all too often is a disgrace.

I find it bizarre that only Wigan and Leeds enjoy undersoil heating, and unforgivably embarrassing that a visiting national team should be asked to play a representative game on a morass of mud and water as happened with the Russians' fixture against British Students at Don-caster in April 1994.

However, all those debates about a salary cap, minimum standards of comfort for spectators, the provision of undersoil heating and so on were brought to a shuddering halt in April 1995 by Rupert Murdoch's plan to take over the exclusive right to televise British Rugby League for five years on his Sky Sports channel for the startling sum of £77 million.

There was no doubt at all when I wrote this chapter that the game was desperate for money, had been on the edge of collapse for a year or more – it was like a starving dog, someone said – and I can forgive the club chairmen for accepting Murdoch's offer and agreeing to set up an international Super League which is what Murdoch allegedly had insisted upon. Then, of course, the real conflicts started. Neither the views of the fans nor the shareholders had been sought (why had the deal to be done so fast?) and it is entirely understandable that the supporters of Castleford, Featherstone Rovers and Wakefield Trinity, for example, bitter long-term local rivals on the field, were incandescent with rage when told that the clubs would have to merge into something called 'Calder' if they were to enjoy a place in the Super League. An additional problem is that the precise terms of the contract with Murdoch have still not been published at the time I write, and so there is no way of knowing if the proposed mergers of a number of clubs was Murdoch's idea or the RFL's way of producing a Super League of the size Murdoch wants.

I think the RFL chairman, Rodney Walker, who is also the chairman of the Sports Council, was being less than fair to the game's supporters when he was reported as having said, 'Only the British seem to have the ability to make unquestionably good news sound like a disaster'. He went on to say, 'It is an opportunity to save the future of the sport leading to a rapid expansion without which we might otherwise have experienced a painful, terminal decline'.

Other crucial aspects of the explosion became apparent as the smoke cleared. In future, Rugby League would become a spring and summer game, running from March to October, a decision which appears to have been more or less universally applauded. Much more serious was the fact that the Australian Rugby League had rejected a similar approach from Murdoch, though Murdoch had countered that by spending an alleged £150 million on buying up not only some clubs in the Winfield Cup but also 120 players to launch a Super League in rivalry to the Australian Rugby League. New Zealand, on the other hand, appear to have surrendered lock, stock and barrel to Murdoch, as have France and PNG. Sadly, the turmoil in Australia will mean the end, at least until the two sides are eventually reconciled, of the long series of Ashes Tests between Great Britain and Australia, although the ARL has agreed to send a team for the centenary World Cup this year.

Predictably, the fight between Murdoch and the ARL was then joined by Kerry Packer whose Australian television channel has the exclusive right to screen ARL matches. The highly respected former Australian coach, Arthur Stanton, was said to have come to Britain on behalf of Kerry Packer offering huge sums of money to a number of British players to bolster Australian clubs. Ellery Hanley of Leeds (said to have been offered £700,000 for a two-year deal) was the first to be targeted, to be followed by Martin Offiah, Jason Robinson and Gary Connolly of Wigan, and doubtless a number of others. However, Offiah, despite a reported offer of £1 million, appears to have been secured for Wigan by an injection of Murdoch money, as have, allegedly, four St Helens internationals. But three weeks after the first announcement of the Super League, the destabilising effect on the game and its supporters, both in this country and in Australia, has been considerable.

In France, too, where Paris will provide one of the Super League clubs, it is said that Jacques Fouroux, France's former Rugby Union coach, is likely to take over the Paris club and will be backed by big investments from French television. Most of the French Rugby Union World Cup squad are rumoured to have agreed to turn professional for Fouroux though their names have not yet been published.

Back in England, the enraged protest lobby succeeded in touching off angry questions in Parliament. Was it right that a media tycoon (and an Australian/American one at that) could acquire a British sport, ironically in its centenary year, irrespective of the feelings of the game's supporters? The protestors demanded that the whole affair should be looked into by the Monopolies and Mergers Commission, which evidently has the power to block such a development. The director-general of the Office of Fair Trading was also asked to exercise his powers to recommend a referral.

All these problems will have been brought to some sort of conclusion by the time this book is published. I just hope that the game survives its ordeal, and is given the stable raft it needs so badly to enable it to go on giving the same pleasure to players and public alike that it has done for a few months short of one hundred years. At least my old club, Workington Town, will be the Cumbrian representative in the Super League.

Then, just after I had written those words, came the news that at a special meeting of clubs in Huddersfield (where the game began ninety-nine years ago) some sort of compromise had been worked out. Now the Super League would consist of twelve clubs (including teams from London and Paris) and there would be a first and second division of eleven and ten clubs respectively. There would be promotion and relegation between the divisions; the idea of mergers between clubs had been abandoned; and Murdoch's purse had been expanded to provide £87 million, with each club in the Super League getting around £900,000 a year for five years; there will be £500,000 a year for each club in the first division and £150,000 a year for each club in the second.

It was also rumoured that Murdoch and Packer were apparently close to some kind of settlement in Australia though that seems not to have prevented the ARL (with Packer's help?) offering Jason Robinson £1.25 million, which he had accepted, binding him to the ARL for four years, though Robinson's current contract keeps him safely at Wigan until 1997. Gary Connolly has also apparently agreed to go to Australia when his present contract is up in 1998. Ellery Hanley, however, has thrown in his lot with the ARL without further delay. While all these negotiations were going on, the RFL, with Murdoch's help, appears to have secured the loyalty of around twenty highly promising young British players by giving them special bonus payments, matching whatever payments Packer was prepared to offer.

Naturally I am delighted that each of the Super League clubs will receive the fabulous sum of £1 million a year for the next five years, with other clubs benefiting also. There is no doubt that, if the money is wisely used, the standards of British Rugby League will be raised. The success of Wigan during this last decade, and to a lesser extent Leeds, is largely because both clubs can afford to pay for full-time professionals, and only with large injections of money can other clubs begin to match Wigan's degree of professionalism.

I am thankful that the smaller clubs are now likely to survive. The roots of Bramley, Batley, Hull Kingston Rovers and Whitehaven – to name only a few – go deep down into their respective communities, with local rivalries so intense that the idea of some of them merging with each other was ridiculous.

And of course I worry that the professional game is now in the hands of a media tycoon who has a generous purse at his disposal but with no guarantee that his generosity will stretch beyond five years. What happens after that?

I feel sorry for Widnes, a club of great achievement over the years, which now finds itself out of the Super League after one poor season. Hull FC, too, who could match any team in the world in their glory years in the 1980s, also now find themselves in the first division rather than the Super League. But they, like Widnes, have the guts to fight back. Keighley Cougars, deined a place in the Super League despite finishing top of the second division at the end of 1994–95, and unaccountably absent when the new plan was put to the vote in Huddersfield, remain in the lower division. All in all, now that the dust has settled, I think the shake-up has been good for the game and has at least provided a new lease of life for a number of clubs, rescued from the edge of bankruptcy.

It has always been the skills and personalities of individual players who have enriched the game for me over the years. Often these days I find myself thinking about those I played with, or have watched since I retired. A number of them I have described at length elsewhere in this book. But if I were to close my eyes now, five players would run towards me. Not all are among the greatest but each has some special quality that appeals to me.

I first met David Watkins in 1987 at a shareholders' dinner at Mansfield Marksman where he was a guest speaker. When I first saw him, I was stunned. This huge star was a midget! He had a glowing record, honours galore and was oozing with talent – and he was gifted with a lovely speaking voice which he used with dignity and self-effacement. He came across like a sober Dylan Thomas.

The next and last time I met him was at the 1993 Wembley Cup final in the VIP lounge. He sat quietly in a corner with two of his friends. I spent a delightful twenty minutes in his company, exchanging anecdotes of our respective rugby careers, oblivious to all the hullaballoo around us, with politicians, industrialists, media and sport people all eating and drinking in festive mood, and discussing how he had felt when he took the giant stride from Union to League.

David still sounded like a Welsh poet, softly spoken, but wonderfully articulate. He reminded me: 'Last time I was here, Cec, I was in the commentators' box. Business and family ties will not allow me time for media commitments now.' His eloquence and analysis of tactics and the strategy of games, and his depth of knowledge from a vast experience of both rugby codes, made him a valuable ambassador for the game beyond its parochial northern environment.

Ray French is a world apart from Eddie Waring but though he is a teacher and a university man, he is a northerner born and bred with the same flat vowels of many of the game's players and administrators. I have always thought that the combination of Ray French and David Watkins would be ideal for putting the game across to an uninitiated southern audience. But now of course David is back in the world of Rugby Union as chairman of Newport in the Heineken Welsh League.

By chance, that same afternoon at Wembley, I encountered a current star, Alan Tait of Leeds. And again by chance I discovered that each

of us had once lived in the same house in Workington. Alan's father
had played Rugby Union for Kelso before signing professional for
Workington in 1967 when Alan was three years old. The family took
possession of the house which had been bought by the club for me
when I first arrived from Hunslet. Then, in 1977, when Alan was
thirteen, the family returned to Kelso where Alan was treated by the
locals as something of an alien since there was no trace of a Scottish
accent in his speech; indeed he speaks broad Cumbrian. He became
depressed and unhappy and turned into something of a recluse. But,
just in time, he joined Kelso rugby club like his father before him and
went on to win four Scottish Rugby Union caps in the 1988 Five
Nations Championship to add to the four he had gained the previous
year in the World Cup. Then Alan decided to repeat his father's career
and turn professional. His father contacted Ike Southward, then the
Cumbrian Rugby League president, who in turn got into touch with
Dougie Laughton, then the Widnes coach, and already famous for
signing Martin Offiah from Rugby Union. Eventually Alan signed for
Widnes for a fee of £85,000 spread over ten years. During his first
season as a professional he won a Great Britain cap – but soon became
aware of his naivety in signing a contract for ten years instead of the
usual three. He asked to see Dougie who renegotiated the contract for
five years. Payment was then made bi-annually *pro rata*; thus, his regular
payments increased from £8,500 to £17,000. However, soon Leeds
(Dougie had moved from Widnes to Leeds) showed a keen interest in
Alan and he eventually signed for them for an unknown fee in 1992,
but this time for three years.

Alan told me, 'At twenty-eight I was becoming increasingly concerned about what I should do when I stop playing. Two years on, I
still think I would like to go into coaching, particularly at Workington.
I left school at fifteen to serve my apprenticeship as a plumber and
eventually joined my dad in business as a builder. I left school without
any qualifications. I hated school.'

This is an area of the game which seriously concerns me. At the
Hunslet reunions I see so many players who have not 'improved'

themselves despite the many opportunities that the game now has to offer. Most have been manual workers and stay that way or move into pubs close by the clubs they played for, displaying on their walls a nostalgic array of photographs of times gone by. I sincerely hope that Alan, who is a good lad, will qualify as a coach and stay in the first-class game. He deserves nothing less.

In January 1994 I bumped into Paul Charlton, a wholehearted Cumbrian if ever there was one, whose rugby career was just beginning as mine was ending, working in a Whitehaven street for the local council. He recognised me at once, 'Eh up, Cec, hows the gaying' on marrer?' Paul was one of the finest full-backs of his time who had played nine outstanding seasons for Workington before being signed by Brian Snape for Salford in 1969–70 for £12,500. With Salford Paul rose to even greater heights and was selected for the Great Britain squad that toured Australia in 1970. Later, in the autumn of his career, he was transferred from Salford back to Workington and in his first season helped to win promotion for his old club from the second to the first division. And not only that, such was Paul's charismatic influence that in the 1977–78 season Workington won the Lancashire Cup for the first and only time in their history, beating Wigan 16–13 at Warrington.

In his years with Salford Paul played brilliantly, forging an unforgettable link with a back division which included such stars as David Watkins, Keith Fielding and Chris Hesketh. He had a wonderful eye for an opening and his breathtaking acceleration as he joined the line enabled him to score numerous sensational tries. Indeed, in 1971–72, he claimed a world record of thirty-three tries for a full-back in a single season.

After we had met, Paul invited me home and we enjoyed a wonderfully nostalgic evening. Seeing Paul in overalls, labouring in that Whitehaven street for the Cumbria CC Highways Department, I had wondered if he had fallen on hard times. But not a bit of it. He had been a skilled carpenter and had worked for several construction companies at Sellafield. There he had been made redundant but had had the good fortune to land his present job, and with the help of a group of fellow craftsmen he had built himself a spacious and comfortable house on the outskirts of Whitehaven, towards St Bees.

On a number of occasions Paul had been tempted to take profitable jobs outside the game: for example, Trevor Green, the managing director of Matthew Brown, the brewers, wanted him to take over the Sunnyhill, a popular public house in Whitehaven with a staff of twelve. But Paul refused since it would have meant giving up coaching youngsters, refereeing their matches and taking their kit home to be washed by his wife, Lily, before turning out for Workington in the afternoon. His love of the game came before riches. Paul had a few games with Blackpool in the twilight of his career; then Australia's sunshine, added to a coaching contract, lured him away down under for three-and-a-half years. He returned to Cumbria to start a series of coaching schemes for Under-9s, Under-11s and Under-13s, organised with Ron Morgan, who writes for the *West Cumbrian Gazette* and at the time was in charge of TV, radio and press relations for Cumbria Rugby League.

When I first met Paul that January morning I was saddened to see that time had helped a great athlete down from the pinnacle of his sport to work as a manual labourer. But that was a sentimental view. Paul now has a house of his own, a far cry from the derelict council estate at Woodhouse where he was born, an estate lost in clouds of smog from the huge chemical plant which hovers over that part of the coast. And of course he is delightfully happy in his dedicated coaching of young players. Needless to say, his present job is pretty grim during the winter when the bitter cold and the Atlantic rainstorms play havoc with his joints: he has had three cartilages removed from his knees. He should still be enjoying that Australian sunshine or at least a less arduous occupation. And I wondered what opportunities to earn more money, with which to make a more emphatic mark on life, must have passed him by, quite apart from that opening with Matthew Brown, during his years of glory. But never mind. Paul will always be one of my heroes and his enthusiasm is enviable, an example to us all.

Now another old friend comes forward. In the opinion of many, Ike Southward was the best rugby winger Cumbria has ever produced and was certainly one of the best wingers ever to have played Rugby League for Great Britain. He was born in the Cumbrian village of Ellenborough in 1934, the youngest of four boys and two girls. His father had played amateur Rugby League and might well have turned professional with Huddersfield but declined trials because, like most Cumbrians at the time, he was not prepared to leave the area. Ike's uncle, Ferguson Southward, on the other hand, played for Salford with Gus Risman and an elder brother played for Whitehaven.

When Ike was at elementary school, a way of earning a few extra pennies in those hard days was to act as a 'pigeon-runner'. Racing pigeons would arrive at a central loft on the village green at Ellenborough, their rings would be taken from their legs and, as there was then only one timing clock, boys would race with the rings to the central clock. The boy who arrived first with the ring was obviously well rewarded by the pigeon owner. Ike first developed his renowned speed down the wing by being one of the runners. In those days he wore clogs instead of rugby boots and many a time fell on the gravel path, eventually developing gravel rash on his knees. The pigeon owner, a man called Jonty Irving, eventually bought the boy a pair of plimsolls to avoid further injury and doubtless to increase his speed still more.

Ike was signed by Gus Risman for Workington Town just before his eighteenth birthday in July 1952, the season before I joined the club. At that time Ike was an apprentice fitter at Wharton's iron foundry at Maryport and soon after signing he was called up to do his national service in the army. Gus pulled all sorts of strings to get Ike home for vital matches, and he was soon playing in the full representative Army side as well, which meant Rugby Union during the week and Rugby

League at weekends. Playing for the Army he scored a memorable try at Twickenham, at the time considered even more remarkable than Prince Obolensky's famous try for England against New Zealand in 1936. Ike also played in two Rugby League Challenge Cup finals and it was Ike who, in the closing minutes of the 1958 final, in which I played and which I have described earlier in this book, might have won the Cup against Wigan if Norman Cherrington had not tapped his ankle just enough to loosen the ball from Ike's grasp as he was about to touch down what would have been the winning try.

Ike had many records to his credit which made him a legend in his lifetime. He was only the third player ever to have scored over 300 tries and 300 goals in a career. He went on two Australasian tours for Great Britain, in 1958 and 1962. On the 1958 tour he played in all three Tests, the second being the famous battle of Brisbane with victory going to Great Britain, who had lost the first Test but went on to win the third. Ike also has the distinction, equalled only by Jonty Parkin (in 1928), of scoring in each Test of that 1958 tour, achieving four tries in all. Ike also helped to win the 1959 Test series in England, playing in the first two, both of which were won by Britain. Altogether he represented Great Britain in eleven Tests and played twelve times for Cumbria. Ike was transferred from Workington to Oldham in 1959 for a then record fee of £10,650 before being transferred back to Workington two years later for £11,000. In a total of 486 games of first-class Rugby League he scored 376 tries and struck 356 goals. Against Blackpool in 1955 he scored no less than seven tries and six goals in the match.

In 1977–78, Workington, now coached by Ike, and with Paul Charlton in the team, won the Lancashire Cup, the only occasion on which the cup has left Lancashire. After he retired, Ike was invited to become a director of Workington, in charge of the ground staff, and he was Cumbria's president in 1990. Today he does a good deal of administrative work for both Workington and Cumbria Rugby League but in his heyday he had opportunities to make a real success of his life outside football but perhaps was not helped or encouraged by the right people. The late Don Revie of Leeds United, when we were fellow members of the BBC Advisory Council in 1970, suggested that facilities should be made available for professional sportsmen to take educational courses when their playing days were over. I thought it was a great idea but sadly nothing came of it.

When I asked Ike why he had never taken advantage of the opportunities to 'better' himself, he replied (I'm translating what he said into English for the sake of comprehension), 'I love my rugby too much and I'm not particularly ambitious. A Workington brewery did offer me a pub, but Betty [his wife] is a strict Methodist and I'm not fond of drink or socialising. I'm happy as I am.'

I once heard that Ike was rather canny with his money. Andy Key and his wife and the Southwards had holidayed together for many years. Andy, like Ike, came from the small village of Ellenborough. They went to school together, both were pigeon-runners and have remained lifetime friends. Andy's wife, Pat, told me a story about Ike with the promise that I would not tell it to anyone else, so I'll keep it to pen and paper.

Andy dreamed that he had drowned off the Cumbrian coast and was delivered, much to his surprise, to the gates of heaven. The gatekeeper, who was an angel, told Andy that he was a marginal case and could not be admitted until he had fully shown his worth. The angel gave Andy an almost impossible task. 'Go down below and move the pyramids.' Andy was powerfully built and extremely strong for his size. Lo and behold, he actually moved the pyramids. Andy came bouncing back to the gates, a huge smile on his face and said, 'Done!' 'Ah,' said the angel, 'just one more simple task. Go down below once more to Workington Town's president's suite. Go to the bar and persuade Ike Southward to buy you a pint.' Andy woke up screaming as flames were about to engulf his body. He was sweating profusely, screaming, 'Southward, you bastard, you bastard . . .' his voice trailing away. Pat almost died of fear, seeing and hearing Andy's desperate situation.

Today, Ike's 10-stone greyhound figure has added another 6 stone or more about which he remarked, 'If tha leaves uh tattie in grund fur lang, iterl turn inta whatter. Uv dun knah runnin fra uh lang time, dutha ken marrer?' I left Ike knowing he was happy and fulfilled. May he long remain so.

Ellery Hanley, on the two occasions I have been in his company, has struck me as an extremely thoughtful and intelligent person. In his heyday, throughout the 1980s, he was ranked as the game's finest player and the most successful post-war British captain. He was a truly charismatic skipper and to captain not only his country but also a club of Wigan's calibre, with its extraordinary array of talented stars, was a feat in itself. And to have such an impact when not fully fit, as was the case in Wigan's 1991 Wembley final against St Helens, makes him a player of almost godlike stature. Certainly Wigan looked on Hanley as a prince of players. But for all this adulation, Ellery, now with Leeds, remains an extremely modest person.

I first met Ellery in my home at Chesterfield in 1986. He came with Phil Larder, who was then the Rugby League's national director of coaching and is now coach at Keighley. Ellery had just qualified as a grade 1 coach with flying colours and he and Larder had come to see me in the hope of fostering closer relations between the Mansfield Marksman professional club, of which I was a director, and the local amateur clubs in the East Midlands area.

I met Ellery for a second time in 1990 after the Wembley final between Wigan and Warrington when he had been awarded the Lance Todd trophy as man-of-the-match. I became even more impressed by this man who is so awesome a professional on the field of play. We met in the VIP lounge after drifting magnetically towards each other to talk privately for some thirty minutes. As we are both teetotallers, we were only too happy to draw away from the noise around us and soon became deeply involved in philosophical discussion about the game and how it has affected our lives. We melted together like Siamese twins, talking without inhibition. Ellery told me that he had had no problems with racism and had been held in respect wherever he played. Sadly for me, Ellery treasures his privacy and so I have not had a chance to see him recently. And anyway I am sure it is fate that dictates when the two of us shall meet.

Since that last Wembley meeting, Ellery has transferred to Leeds, where he has proved to be an even greater charismatic influence than he was at Wigan. And when Malcolm Reilly, the Great Britain coach, left to go to Australia in the autumn of 1994, Ellery was appointed Great Britain coach before the Tests against Australia that autumn. Indeed, he has become truly a world personality during the last eight or nine years when the game has won for itself – at any rate in Britain and Australia – the highest profile it has ever enjoyed. He is also the player whom Kerry Packer first targeted when looking for personalities in this country to boost the Australian League during the extraordinary happenings which rocked the game in the spring of 1995. Now he has left for Australia and the British game will be the poorer for his absence.

Ellery is a man of considerable intelligence, and possibly his honorary degree from Leeds Polytechnic (now a university) may nudge him towards formalising his mental ability in some way. Ellery's strength of character made him the perfect captain of the national side, before he was appointed the Great Britain coach, although, perhaps through jealousy, many were annoyed by the award of his MBE in 1990.

Many of the parochial, narrow-minded administrators of the game seem to overlook the fact that some players are transformed by the sport; they experience a sort of metamorphosis, becoming different people with different aspirations, different aims in life. If the administrators cannot accept this fact then they have little understanding of life and of human nature. Just as I found myself transformed into a teacher and a not unsuccessful business man, it is perfectly possible that Ellery will be transformed when his playing and coaching days are over, and I wonder what new worlds he will be ready to conquer then. An outstanding coach he has already proved himself to be but what else may lie in store for him?

I've said elsewhere in this book that I need to be able to earn enough money to travel freely whenever I want to and to whatever destination – within reason anyway. Certainly the travels I have undertaken during the years when funds have allowed me that luxury have had an almost magical effect on me. Two of the first journeys Anne and I made together were to Austria, on one occasion taking in the Oberammagau passion play. Then at the end of my second year at Leeds I took advantage of the university's facilities for student holidays, going off with Anne to Greece for six weeks. No holiday has meant more to me. Most of the students arrived at Dover to board a train from Ostend to Yugoslavia; half the train and its passengers went to Istanbul, the other half to Athens. The services aboard the train were spartan, which meant hasty purchases of wine, fruit, bread and cheese from stations when the train stopped for fuel. But though the facilities were pretty basic it was wonderful to be among those students, many of whom were reading classics at university. So was I, in a way. A friend had lent me Leonard Cotterell's *The Bull of Minos* and the story of the Minoan civilisation and the Palace of Knossos has remained vividly in my mind to this day.

I found myself – with my orphanage upbringing and working-class background – surrounded by bookish, cultured young people, mostly from middle-class homes. They were either unaware of the differences between us, or politely put them down to my different coloured skin, but I was acutely self-conscious. It wasn't that I was black: that was easily overlooked. I felt I was placed between two cultures and just did not belong in the one in which I found myself. I believed I had been artificially elevated through my minor educational achievements at college and brief spell at university and would never be on a par with those youngsters. Actually it was as well that those gifted young people were there. Any problems I encountered with *The Bull of Minos* were easily resolved with so many classical students around me.

Our hotel was on a hill top and meals were taken on the roof, so we were almost parallel with the ruins of the Acropolis. I had seen posters of Knossos and the Parthenon in classrooms when I was cleaning windows, and in my naval days I had passed through the Mediterranean on my way to the Far East, but this was entirely different. Until recently I had no knowledge at all of the history of this part of the world, indeed of no other part of the Mediterranean come to that, and suddenly the world was available to me in a way it had never been before.

From Greece we went to Crete and there we met Roger and Sally Majak, an American couple who have remained good and constant friends. On one unforgettable occasion we went to see them in Washington DC and there the prize I had been awarded at speech day in Huddersfield in 1963, the Abraham Lincoln book, came alive for me. My imagination, as I looked out from the four observation windows at the top of the Washington monument, clothed it with flesh and blood, and like a child working through a general knowledge paper I devoured all that Roger had to say about the history of the United States. From Washington we went on to the Blue Ridge Mountains, as beautiful and compelling as the Lake District; to Williamsburg; and then to Richmond. If Williamsburg was the past, Richmond, with a population of a third of a million, seemed very much of the present. As the four of us walked down one of the main shopping streets, every face we saw seemed to be black. I felt unnerved. Partly this was something we picked up from Roger and Sally, who also seemed not to feel at home there. But Anne and I, though equally unaccustomed to such an environment, should surely have felt at ease. But of course I am no more used to seeing blacks in large numbers than any other Englishman of my generation.

Another close friendship that sprang from that same long holiday in Greece was with a girl called Jamie, from New York University, who was there with a party of fellow graduates. She was directly responsible for three more wonderful holidays. Twice we went to see her family in Philadelphia and in 1971 we visited her and her new husband in Algiers. I recently faxed Jamie from Ambler, Philadelphia, seeking her views on how our friendship had developed and matured. This is what she replied:

Well, we met by serendipity, through a close desire to see Greece and the wine dark sea. I remember the boat and the seasickness, our swim to the picnic from the boat and the uninhabited island. Anne was such a happy one, with her white teeth and pale eyes, and your relationship fascinated me because you seemed so different. For me, friendship starts with curiosity and wonder because without them what is there to hang around for anyway. And friendship is such an ephemeral thing, existing only in the electric currents in our brains.

I remember the visit to your home very well, better than your visit to us in Algeria. I remember your house and your cooker in your kitchen, and the long back garden. We went climbing in the Lake District, looking down at Windermere from a height, marvelling at its beauty. You shared your wonders with me unstintingly. Did we reciprocate when you came to Algiers? Are your memories alive from that time? All I really remember is that when you came back from Tamanrasset, over 1,000 miles across the Algerian Sahara, you said that you had never valued water so much, or realised its importance.

Now we have both got families. Morad graduates from high school soon; the twins are seventeen. Time moves on, so why is it then that some friendships stay alive through distance and time and neglect, only needing a note or Christmas card to keep them going, whereas other friendships, despite proximity, decline and fade? I can only assume, Cec, it is because we are both rather unorthodox (and, though I shouldn't say it, both very smart).

We had visited her in Philadelphia shortly after Martin Luther King's assassination. I was only too aware of the need to tread carefully. A lot of issues were being thrown around like confetti at the time, and old loyalties were being challenged. I need not to have worried. We were treated everywhere like royalty. Jamie's friends in New York took us round Manhattan and Coney Island and the next stop was Philadelphia where we discovered that Jamie's father was a millionaire. She might have warned us! We were met at the airport by a Cadillac which was ours for ten days and were put up in self-contained accommodation. We were treated like film stars.

When we went to see Jamie in Algiers it was the turn of Anne to get used to being stared at because of the colour of her skin. In the Atlas mountains there is a tribe whose skin is so black it has a blue tint to it, and though there are many various shades as one descends from the mountains to the coast, Anne's Cumbrian white wasn't one of them. She was so white she looked like an Eskimo and so received the constant curious attention of the indigenous population. I walked away from her in case anyone thought she was with me!

It was on that visit that we drove across the Algerian Sahara, travelling the 1,000 miles due south to the oasis at Tamanrasset, which Jamie had mentioned in her fax to me. At times the temperature rose to 140 degrees in the shade. We travelled in stretches of 200–300 miles and saw only the odd nomad between oases or the occasional family camped in the middle of a sand dune. We made the journey with a group of French tourists – Anne and I were the only English people – and our hotel in Tamanrasset was magical under a clear and star-studded sky: silence, a full moon, and one another's company.

Back in Algiers we made friends with a young Algerian teacher of English. She begged us to go to her home in the Casbah where she offered us wonderful hospitality. Surrounded by squalor, her home was clean and orderly, elegant like herself. What would she have made of Windermere, I wondered, had she, like Jamie, been able to visit us there? That friendship, I am afraid, was one that did not last. Indeed, I often wonder where she is today. Has she become a victim of Moslem rectitude? Would she dare to introduce two Britishers to the Casbah, to her home, today? Have her warm and generous feelings for the

West prevailed against religious orthodoxy? I pray she has not suc-
cumbed.

Then in 1989, sixty-three long years since my father's death, I journeyed
at last to the place where he was born. Thanks to Ray Battison, who
had been the swimming instructor at Chesterfield, and is a dedicated
amateur genealogist, I knew at least something about my father's family.
After months of patient research, Ray had discovered that my father
was born in 1887 at 81 Queen Street, Port of Spain, which, we
discovered, is close to the parliament building. This at least was a
starting point and also something of a relief. I had worried a little about
what I might find. But apparently my father's family had a certain
amount of status, and my grandparents had been respectable and
married. I already knew, of course, that my father had reached the
rank of corporal in the West Indies Regiment and, because he was
black, that was as far as he could get: commissions were for whites
only.

Until just before our visit, I had assumed that Trinidad was a sort
of backwater, and I had been approaching the holiday with something
of the smug superiority a Victorian Englishman might have felt. But
a few days before setting off I had read the obituary in the *Independent*
of that great Trinidadian, C. L. R. James. At the time I knew nothing
of James – historian, novelist, prophet of Pan-Africanism, philosopher
and cricket writer – but within two hours of reading the obituary I
had taken his book *Black Jacobins* from the library. Here was a man of
learning using his knowledge to illuminate his people's past, and I had
the uncomfortable suspicion that his diversified talents must in some
way testify to the rich culture of his native land. But I still did not
know what to expect when we landed.

Donna Carter met us at the airport. It was soon clear to me how
strange Donna must have found England and the taxi driver's prejudice,
for at home in Trinidad we saw her treated with the utmost deference.

However, if England seemed odd to her, Trinidad was equally strange
to me. It may have been the place my father had come from, where
my roots are, but it really didn't touch me. While it was wonderful
to stand at the very spot in Port of Spain where my father had been
born, at the same time the island was too different, too alien to mean
anything to me directly. There seemed to be so much happiness, yet
so much poverty. There were lots of rich and highly educated people
there, but far more who were desperately poor. An economist by
training, I could only wonder at what had happened to the huge profits
made from the island's sugar industry. They certainly hadn't been used
to supply public facilities: houses, roads, education. It was apparent,
and marvellous, that racism had disappeared, but the class system that
had emerged in its place seemed just as divisive.

I have to add that I found my own situation there a bit perplexing.
I was completely anonymous, just another black face in a sea of black
faces. Rugby League is hardly known on this island off the Venezuelan
coast of South America, so I gained no kudos from that part of my
career. Having a degree gave me no distinction whatever: the Caribbean
middle classes have a fetish about education and for such a small island
there is a disproportionate number of private schools, doctors of philosophy and Oxbridge graduates. In short, my achievements counted
for nothing. In Britain, I may be thought of in some way as unique,
yet in my father's less developed country I could claim no distinction.

I busied myself for the first few days searching for my roots. But it
was tedious, fruitless work, and to continue would have spoilt the
holiday for Anne and Mark, so I abandoned my quest. I had gone to
Trinidad, hoping finally to pin down my identity and establish who I
am, but it had not worked out like that. But still, though I was certainly
no longer unique in any way at all, we found ourselves fêted. This
was due entirely to the warmth and friendship of the Trinidadian
people. I have never known such hospitality. We were guests at a
fashionable wedding reception, invited to plantation homes straight out
of *Gone with the Wind*, and went scuba-diving among the breathtaking
flora and fauna of the seabed off Tobago.

But while this made for a splendid holiday, it wasn't what I had been looking for. In fact, I found myself glad to return to the grey, drab United Kingdom. For all its dreadful damp winters and its unpredictable summers, it is still my home. We Britishers tend to take each other for granted, but I still find that the British are among the finest if not the finest people of all.

Yet, as C. L. R. James testifies, I have no shame about my West Indian heritage. James was born in 1901 in Tunapuna, the very village where Donna Carter lives and where we stayed. He was well educated in Trinidad. He had an encyclopaedic knowledge of English literature and history, a command of Latin and Greek, and an obsessive interest in the Caribbean, from its remote history to its contemporary cricket heroes. *The Black Jacobins* is about Toussaint L'Ouverture and his revolution which started in 1791 in Haiti, at the time a French colony. The French were proud of Haiti: half a million slaves worked there, making huge profits for their masters. When France was torn by revolution, the slaves, led by Toussaint, seized their chance to rebel. By 1801 Toussaint controlled not only Haiti but the whole island of Hispaniola.

However, Napoleon, who had publicly stated that he hated 'niggers', sent an army to subdue the rebels. Toussaint was arrested and died, horribly, in a French prison. But the people of Haiti managed to retain the independence they had won in 1801. Haiti is not a model republic. Many atrocities have happened there over the years. But it was the first to achieve its independence, and, like James, I salute it for that. Now of course all the Caribbean islands are independent. Their regiments no longer have white officers, their cricket teams white captains. For the first time in my life I felt proud of being half Trinidadian.

I had thought myself to be on my way to a poor backward island, where I would be seen as something of a celebrity, a high achiever. I was proved to be very happily mistaken. Yet despite the rich culture of the islands, the greatest marvel in my ancestry has to be the courage and character of my parents. What amazingly strong people those two, William Thompson and Florence Greenwell, must have been. To have

met and to have fallen in love was nothing exceptional perhaps, but
to have endured the inevitable taunts for the sake of their love: that
must have been something.

So there is a sense in which my story, interesting though it may be,
is but an echo of their story, and how I wish I knew their story better.
Instead, I can claim knowledge of only a few facts, a few hints, and a
couple of locations on different sides of the Atlantic. Yet perhaps, after
all, that is enough. I could not choose my parents nor the circumstances
of my birth, but my mixed blood has done me no harm. I am Theodore
Cecil Thompson, half Trinidadian, by upbringing half a Yorkshireman,
proud of both. I am a graduate of Leeds University, a businessman by
trade, a teacher by profession. I have a wonderful son who takes things
for granted and a wonderful wife who thinks she is taken for granted.
And, like Othello, another black man in a white man's world, I believe
I have done the state some service. I would have it no other way.

Afterword

BY WILLIS HALL

Theofore Cecil Thompson is the sort of chap who, in a straight two-man contest at ebullient opportunism, would streak effortlessly past the post leaving Arnold Bennett's 'Card' gasping halfway down the track. Cec Thompson is one of those infuriating and yet engaging fellows who make as much advantage out of life's 'downs' as they are granted by its 'ups'.

As a pointer to how hard it was, with Cec Thompson's background, to grow up, in the late 1930s, in the uncompromising Leeds back-streets, it is sigfnificant to note that, in comparison, he can describe his time spent in a no-nonsense, no-frills orphanage as being 'like paradise'.

Personally speaking, I am as pleased as Punch at having been witness to Cec's early days. In the far-off times of my South Leeds childhood, in our back-to-back two-up-one down, my parents and I looked forward keenly to a weekly incident. Every Saturday morning a tall black youth strode jauntily along our cobbled street. Black men were so scarce in Hunslet (the Leeds suburb where I grew up), that we rushed to the window, twitched the net-curtain, and watched the young man go past. The same thing happened, I am sure, at every window along that street.

In later years, I was to realise that we had been privileged to see the young Cec Thompson bound for his factory bench. By which time, Cec was playing Rugby League not only for Hunslet (a team which I have supported faithfully, if at a distance, for over fifty years) but also for his county and his country.

When Cec signed for Hunslet, for the then not inconsiderable sum of £250, he had only ever played rugby three times in his life before and his entire knowledge of the rules of the game consisted of 'Don't kick the ball and never pass it forward'. But what Hunslet paid good money for – and be sure that Hunslet never chucked money needlessly about – was Cec Thompson's dogged and unbounded enthusiasm. Ask anyone who played with him or, more pertinently perhaps, against him. Certainly no player has proved a finer credit to the game of Rugby League.

As a Great Britain player, Cec was embarrassed when his meagre writing abilities limited him to printing his name in autograph-books. Forced into mastering 'joined-up' writing, it was no more than typical of Cec that he should turn that skill to greater advantage by dubbing himself a journalist and taking on two weekly sporting columns for two separate Rugby League magazines.

Spurred into further self-improvement, Cec read his way along library shelves, progressed through night-school, then college, eventually acquiring an honours degree at Leeds University – all of which would have been achievement enough, but at the same time he subsidised his education working as a window-cleaner – a one-man business which, over the years, he has built into a large and prosperous organisation with himself as managing director.

Successful businessman; lecturer in economics; ex-international rugby player with a keen and time-consuming involvement in student rugby, Cec Thompson, now in his late sixties, still finds time to play tennis every day. I don't know how he does it! Yes, I do – with a dogged and unbounded enthusiasm for life itself. It comes as no surprise that he has written this warm and richly rewarding book – I am only curious to learn why he has not attempted it sooner . . .

Half a century and more have slipped away since I hurried to the window, as a child, to watch the black man walk down our street. These days I am both pleased and proud to have Cec Thompson for a friend. There is nothing nicer than to have lunch with Cec and to talk until the cows come home about Rugby League, literature, society, music, the theatre, politics, art, philosophy – you name it.

And, who knows, one of these fine days I might myself succeed in getting a word in edgeways.

Appendix

CEC THOMPSON'S CAREER
IN RUGBY LEAGUE, 1948–1962

HUNSLET	Debut: 20 Nov. 1948 *v.* Hull KR (home); lost 8–10	
	Appearances	*Tries*
1948–49	10	0
1949–50	10	0
1950–51	16	3
1951–52	33	3
1952–53	27	3
TOTALS	96	9
	Last game 18 April 1953 *v.* Halifax (away); lost 5–21	

WORKINGTON TOWN	Debut: 15 Aug. 1953 *v.* Dewsbury (away); won 30–12, scored 1 try	
	Appearances	*Tries*
1953–54	42	9
1954–55	18	9
1955–56	25	12
1956–57	36	3
1957–58	38	13
1958–59	17	3
1959–60	15	6
1960–61	1	0
TOTALS	192	55
	Last game 19 Sept. 1960 *v.* Bradford Northern (home); won 28–2	

BARROW	*Appearances*	Tries
1960–61	0	0
1961–62	2	0
TOTALS	2	0

REPRESENTATIVE MATCHES

6 Oct. 1951	Great Britain	21	New Zealand	15	at Odsal Stadium, Bradford
10 Nov. 1951	Great Britain	20	New Zealand	19	at Swinton
19 May 1952	Empire XIII	29	Welsh XIII	16	at Llanelli
22 Oct. 1959	Workington Town/ Whitehaven	8	Australians	13	at Workington

CAREER TOTALS

294 games   64 tries

All Cec's games for Hunslet and in representative matches were as a second-rower. For Workington he played all his 192 games as a second rower except for twenty-two at loose forward and six on the wing. At Barrow, with the side plagued by injury, he played two games as a second-rower, against Bramley and Blackpool, to make up numbers.

Subscribers

Bill Abernethy, Brisbane,
Queensland

Dr Jack Abernethy OBE,
Cockermouth

Wilbur & Rita Abersmith,
Ulverston

I. A. Ackroyd, Halifax

Eric Allison, Cockermouth

Wynne & Bill Anderston,
Addingham, Yorkshire

Carol Armstrong, Workington

Mr & Mrs F. Armstrong,
Cockermouth

Harry Armstrong, Cockermouth

Patricia Arthur, Birkenhead

Dr Janak & Margaret Asher,
Chesterfield

Anne Atkinson, Lincoln

Alasdair Auld, Sutton-in-Ashfield

John Auld, Sutton-in-Ashfield

Edward M. Baker, Leeds

Paul J. Bamford, Chesterfield

Derrick Barber, Chesterfield

Paul John Barron, Chesterfield

Hazel & Glenys Barson, South
Normanton, Derbyshire

Fred Bartlett, Hosforth, Leeds

Pat Beamish, Formby

Dr Madhukar K. Bedarkar, Reading

Mrs K. A. Bell, Workington

Professor Maurice Beresford, Leeds
University

Miss M. Bewley, Maryport

Elizabeth Bhoomkar, Chesterfield

Doug Billings, Leeds

Mark Bointon, Leicester

Nigel Brackenbury, Chesterfield

Andrew Branthwaite, Keswick

Richard K. Broadhead, Tunbridge
Wells

Neil Brown, Chesterfield

Ron Brown, Leeds

John F. Brothwell, Wetherby

David Brucklow, Chesterfield

Alf 'Ginger' Burnell, Leeds

Mrs Jeanne Burt, Chesterfield

Andrew M. Butler, Chesterfield

Mr & Mrs M. Butterworth,
Workington

J. R. Cairns, Workington

Duncan Calow, London

Daryl Camm, Chesterfield

Ted Carroll, Ilkley

M. T. Carruthers, Workington

Lee F. Carson, Ossett

Thomas Caton, Egremont

Professor John Chartres, Leeds
University

Maurice Clarke, Maryport

Ed & Eileen Cockran, Macclesfield

Ian Coleman, Leeds

Richard & Michael Coleman,
Chesterfield

Tony Collins, Leeds

Stephen Crelling, Workington

Dr Murray & Shirley Cresswell,
Gorleston, Norfolk

Lynne & Brian Crook, Chesterfield

Andrew Cudbertson, Gorsedd,
　Clwyd
Russell & Sarah Currins,
　Swanwick, Derbyshire
Paul W. H. Curtis, Chesterfield
Paul Dart, Chesterfield
Peter Dawson, Chesterfield
Robert Donkin, Bradford
Jon Dowham, Chesterfield
Professor Claude & Andre Duluc,
　France
Sue & Dick East, London
Clive Edwards, Chesterfield
Sheila Ellis, Manchester
Sid Ellis, London
Maurice Eve, Flimby, Maryport
Albert Eyre, Leeds
Mrs. M. Ferguson, Workington
Gordon Ferguson, Workington
Ashley Firn, Cockermouth
Mark Fitzpatrick, Mapperley,
　Nottingham
Paul Foster, Chesterfield
Christina Galbraith, Chesterfield
Mike Gardner, Barrow-in-Furness
Robert Gate, Sowerby Bridge
D & A George, Perugia, Italy
Jim Gilmartin, Wetherby
Gary & David Gorman,
　Chesterfield
David Godfrey, Chesterfield
Kavin Goodwin, Chesterfield
Dorothy Graves, Cockermouth
Mike Green, Leeds
J. D. Greenhough, Wakefield
Nigel Greenway, Chesterfield
Adam F. Griffiths, Illinois, USA
Alan Hall, Workington
Colin Hall, Workington

Willie Hall, Ilkley
Ellery Hanley MBE, Leeds
Kevin Hansen, Warrington
Dean Harper, London
Brian Harrison, Bradford
David Harrison, Chesterfield
Lilian Harrison, Castleford
Maggie Hewitt, Leeds
Michael & Shirley Hogan,
　Workington
Joe Holliday, Workington
Ian Hollis, Chesterfield
Les Hoole, Drighlington, Yorkshire
Roy Hoodless, Derby
Syd Hutchinson, Cockermouth
James Irving, Maryport
Bill Ivill, Pontefract
Mr & Mrs Harry Jepson,
　Rothwell, Leeds
Niall Johnson, Chesterfield
Jeremy Jones, Chesterfield
Joan & Eric Kari, Ontario, Canada
Bob & Chris Kenna, Scayne's Hill,
　Sussex
Peter Kennan, Chesterfield
Jos Kenley, Dalton-in-Furness,
　Cumbria
Andy Key, Workington
John & Tandy Kinglake,
　Rickmansworth
Robin Kirk, Keswick
G. H. Lewthwaite, Whitehaven
Dr Roy Lewis, Baslow, Derbyshire
Amanda Little, Carlisle
Tom Little, Cockermouth
James T. Livsey, Christchurch
Roger M. Livsey, Chesterfield
Tom Lock, Workington
Gerhard & Ruth Lohaus, Germany

Peter Lush, London
Philip Mackay, Flimby, Maryport
Peter McVeigh, Batley
Roger & Sally Majak, Washington
    DC, USA
D. C. Makin, Leeds
C. W. Martin, Whitehaven
Joan Martin, Workington
Patricia Martin, Workington
Harold & Pat Mellors, Chesterfield
Ian T. Messenger, Workington
J. Eric Milburn, Workington
R. Miles, Cockermouth
Canon F. Moore, Seaton, Cumbria
Ann Morton, Stockport
Dennis Murphy, Pudsey
Bill Nelson, Cleator Moor
Netherhall School, Maryport
Norman Nicholson, Workington
Jamie Nouri, Philadelphia, USA
Ralph 'Olly' Ormondroyd, Leeds
T. Ousby, Workington
David Oxley OBE, Harrogate
Mrs A. Plamer, Corby
Reg Parker, Grange-over-Sands,
    Cumbria
Roy Parkin, Barrow-upon-Humber
Mark Peel, Edinburgh
Jean & John Pharoah, Carlisle
Polyanna & Anna Louise
    Pickering, Matlock, Derbyshire
Mike & Pam Pitcher,
    Buckinghamshire
Kate Pocock, London
Tony Pocock, London
Darren Pollitt, Windsor
Dr Vad Prakash, Secunderabad,
    India
Dr Udai Prakash, Edinburgh

Derrick Priestley, Chesterfield
Peter Price, Workington
Corrado Risino, Workington
N. H. Ratcliffe, Egremont
Bill Riley, BFPO 30
Bev Risman, Crowthorne,
    Berkshire
John Riseman, Cockermouth
John L. Roberts, Chesterfield
Richard & Jill Robinson,
    Chesterfield
Rachel & Shantaat Robinson,
    Leicester
Ken Rollin, Wakefield
Sid Rookes, Aberford, Leeds
Yvonne Rosier, Beddington, Surrey
James Routledge, Maryport
St Josephs School, Workington
Martha Salisbury, Workington
Matthew E. Savage, Chesterfield
Dennis Scholes, Hull
Roger S. Shackleton, Hebden
    Bridge
Budge Alan Simpson, Leeds
Trevor Skerritt, Leeds
Alan Smith, Mirfield, Yorkshire
Ike Southward, Workington
Andrew Spencer, Oxford
Karl Spracklen, Bramley, Leeds
Ted Steele, Workington
Robert M. Stevenson, Chesterfield
Jim Sullivan, Cleator Moor
Terry Swift, Batley, Yorkshire
Arthur Talbot, Dewsbury
Jenny Tasker, St Peter Port,
    Guernsey
Brian Taylor, Flimby, Maryport
Duncan Taylor, Alfreton
Ewart Taylor, Chesterfield

Robert Thompson, Leeds
J. R. Thwaites, Whitehaven
Michael Toth, Clay Cross,
    Derbyshire
Laurie & Rose Trickett, Leeds
Neil Tunnicliffe, Harrogate
Ron Turner, Hull
D. G. Vallett, St Helens
Philippa Varah, Cockermouth
Joe Vickers, Maryport
Dick Viney, Kendal
Jack Walkington, Hosforth, Leeds
Jonathan R. Wall, Chesterfield
Richard and John Wardle,
    Chesterfield
Mike Walter, Chesterfield
Roy Waudby, Hull
Phil & Joy Webb, Chesterfield
D. West, Harrow

West Cumberland College Library,
    Workington
Mary & Harry White, Workington
Ian Whitley, Chesterfield
Professor Roy Wilkinson, Sheffield
    University
M. B. Wilkinson, Chesterfield
Ian M. Williams, Colchester
Les Williams, Penryn
Brian Wilshaw, Workington
Steve Williams, Workington
Bev Wilson, French Forest, New
    South Wales
Mr & Mrs J. R. Woodhall,
    Warley, West Midlands
Doreen Wodward, Castleford
Derek Wyatt, London
Graham Yapp, Chesterfield